Home STORAGE *projects*

Creative Solutions for Every Room in the House

PAUL ANTHONY

The Taunton Press

Text © 2002 by Paul Anthony

Photographs © 2002 by Paul Anthony, except pp. iv, 2, 22, 32, 42, 54, 68, 80, 88, 94, 108, and 158 © Rich Bienkowski; p. 128 © Greg Browning; and pp. 1 and 138 © Dennis Griggs

Illustrations © 2002 by The Taunton Press, Inc.

The Taunton Press
Inspiration for hands-on living™

The Taunton Press, Inc., 63 South Main Street, PO Box 5506, Newtown, CT 06470-5506
e-mail: tp@taunton.com

Distributed by Publishers Group West

INTERIOR DESIGN AND LAYOUT: Lori Wendin
COVER DESIGN: Ann Marie Manca
ILLUSTRATOR: Ron Carboni
COVER PHOTOGRAPHERS: Rich Bienkowski (front cover), Paul Anthony (back cover), and Jean Anthony (author photo)

LIBRARY OF CONGRESS CATALOGING-IN-PUBLICATION DATA:
Anthony, Paul.
    Home storage projects : creative solutions for every room in the house / Paul Anthony.
        p. cm.
    ISBN 1-56158-498-3
    1. Cabinetwork--Amateurs' manuals. 2. Furniture making--Amateurs' manuals. 3. Storage in the home--Amateurs' manuals. I. Title.
TT197 .A54 2001
684.1'6--dc21   2001053513

Printed in the United States of America
10 9 8 7 6 5 4 3 2 1

WORKING WITH WOOD IS INHERENTLY DANGEROUS. Using hand or power tools improperly or ignoring safety practices can lead to permanent injury or even death. Don't try to perform operations you learn about here (or elsewhere) unless you're certain they are safe for you. If something about an operation doesn't feel right, don't do it. Look for another way. We want you to enjoy the craft, so please keep safety foremost in your mind whenever you're in the shop.

To my sweet Jeanie, without whom it wouldn't have been possible.

ACKNOWLEDGMENTS

AS WITH MOST BOOKS, this one was the result of work by a lot of different people. First of all, I would like to thank Helen Albert at Taunton Press for her encouragement and assistance in focusing and getting this book into gear. Strother Purdy also deserves much credit for his instigations and advice. But the person who really deserves special credit is my editor, Tom Clark. I'm very grateful for his patience and guidance.

A sincere thanks to all of the woodworkers who contributed projects for this book: Ken Burton, Denis Kissane, Adolph Schneider, Allen Spooner, and Peter Turner. Special kudos to Ken and Adolph for going the extra mile when I needed it. I also appreciate the folks who submitted wonderful designs that didn't make it into the book because of space constraints. Thanks to photographer Richard Bienkowski for the wonderful photos of the finished projects.

For behind-the-scenes assistance, consultation, and friendship, I want to acknowledge my woodworker/ writer cohorts Dave Freedman, Andy Rae, Dave Sellers, David Sloan, Tim Snyder, Joe Wajszczuk, and Ellis Walentine. All helped shape my woodworking and writing skills.

Of course my family has helped pay the price for producing this book. My love and gratitude to Jeanie, Emily, Mary Lou, and Al for their personal sacrifices and encouragement as I sweated this book out. And last but certainly not least, I owe a debt of gratitude to my parents, sisters, brother, and son for all the love and lessons over the years.

You're all in this book, in one way or another.

CONTENTS

INTRODUCTION

STUFF. We humans are magnets for it. Everyday life seems to require a cornucopia of accessories—from bed linens, clothes, and food to books, office supplies, and computer equipment. And that doesn't include all of the other collectibles that we're so fond of, including jewelry, music equipment, toys, and curios. The price of all this stuff, of course, is that it all has to live somewhere. And it needs to be accessible and organized or you'll waste hours of your life digging around for things buried in boxes or piled in corners.

But not to worry. Even if your home is beginning to resemble a frat house, there are plenty of good solutions for cleaning up the clutter. In this book you'll find thirteen cleverly designed projects for organizing and storing your belongings. And we're not talking closet shelving here; these are furniture-quality pieces that you'll be proud to display in your home as a products of your own handiwork.

The projects in this book reflect a variety of styles and draw on the design expertise of some of the best woodworkers in the country. The designs range from simple to ambitious, and any of them can be modified to suit your particular needs. Some, like the pantry door shelves and CD cabinet can be built in less than a day. Others, like the audiocassette cabinet and wine cabinet could probably be knocked out in a weekend. More involved projects such as the storage bench and kitchen work station may take a week or more, depending on how fussy you are about construction and finish quality. In any case, all of the projects are well within the reach of any determined woodworker with a basic complement of tools.

In the process of building the projects, you'll also learn a lot about woodworking. Each chapter includes great information on techniques, tools, joinery, and finishing. You'll discover better ways to lay out and cut joints, fit drawers, and clamp up work. Never tried resawing or veneering? You'll find out how easy it can be. You'll also learn how to make clever jigs that will serve you in future woodworking projects.

Just as important, you'll learn how to design your own storage furniture. The first chapter walks you through the steps of assessing your particular storage problems and of developing appropriate solutions. Among other things, it discusses sizing furniture to maximize storage, matching or complementing existing decor, tailoring a piece to suit its location, and making the most of available space.

So have at it. You'll enjoy making these pieces. They'll beautify your home and make your life more efficient and enjoyable. After all, the more organized your things are, the more space you'll create for comfort (or, of course, for more stuff!).

You can take the basic plan of any project and modify it to match your existing capacity needs and decor. This kitchen base cabinet is an upsize version of the small wine cabinet on p. 80.

DESIGNING AND BUILDING STORAGE PROJECTS

ESIGNING FOR STORAGE can be both a curse and a blessing. On the one hand, the immense design possibilities can seem overwhelming: You can make cabinets, boxes, bins, or benches and outfit them with dividers, shelves, drawers, doors, or racks. On the other hand, you often have the advantage of designing around items' specific sizes and shapes, which can give you a focus and a good running start. If you carefully consider the particular items to be stored and the space that the finished project will occupy, you've got half the battle won.

In this book, you'll find projects for use throughout the home—from the living room and office to the kitchen, bedroom, and bathroom. Some of the projects have been carefully designed to maximize storage for particular objects such as CDs, cassette tapes, wine bottles, and office files. Other projects, such as the kitchen work station (p. 94), bed pedestal (p. 108), printer stand (p. 54), and storage bench (p. 138) offer great versatility for general household and office storage.

Most of the pieces in this book should work great for you just as they are. However, you may want to customize some of them to suit your personal needs. In some cases, you'll want to change the size of a design to accommodate your specific collection of items. Sometimes, you'll want to modify the dimensions to suit a certain space in your house or apartment.

Planning and Customizing Designs

When it comes to designing, begin with what you know. Note the dimensions of the objects to be stored. If you are dealing with a standard size, as for CDs and file folders, design around that size to minimize wasted space. For example, a cabinet for audiotapes should accommodate the cassettes while leaving just enough space for finger access.

In some cases, you can't be sure what the finished project will hold. The kitchen work station, for example, needs to be able to store a variety of things. In that case, it's wise to build in as much flexibility as possible, incorporating drawers and cabinets of different dimensions. Drawers provide great storage because they'll hold so many different items while keeping them clean and accessible, but out of sight. Cabinets are easy to build and can be used to display your collections if you don't install doors. When designing different size drawers and compartments in a single piece, it's aesthetically best if they graduate in size from the small-

Organizing Compartments

When designing compartments, consider storage for transitional items as well as for those needing permanent storage. Ken Burton's desktop organizer (p. 42) provides a good example of thoughtful design. It includes an in/out box, dividers for active files, bins for paper, and drawers for computer disks.

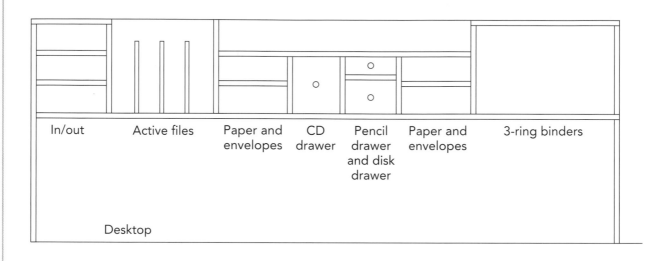

In/out | Active files | Paper and envelopes | CD drawer | Pencil drawer and disk drawer | Paper and envelopes | 3-ring binders

Desktop

est at the top to the largest at the bottom. Also, don't forget to plan for transitional items, such as paperwork in process, or for temporary storage for items that will eventually be tossed or distributed (see "Organizing Compartments").

Customizing the Size of Your Project

You can change the overall size of any project in this book to alter its storage capacity. Sometimes, you'll need to maintain certain compartment dimensions; but other than that, you've got a lot of room to play.

For example, the audiocassette cabinet (p. 32) could easily be made wider or taller, as long as you maintain the height and depth of the individual compartments. Similarly, although the width of the drawers in the file cabinet (p. 68) must be maintained, you can build the drawers to the length of the drawer slides you choose. Or you can make the cabinets three or four drawers tall. The desktop organizer (p. 42) should certainly be sized to fit its desk, even if that means modifying the size or arrangement of the individual compartments.

Designing to fit a particular space

If you're building a piece to suit a particular space, you'll want to fit the space visually. But don't forget to consider the negative space in the whole picture. For example, if you're making a cabinet to stand against a particular section of wall, you may not want to span the entire width of the section but, instead, leave a bit of room on either side and above to create a visual frame of sorts.

Often, you may want to match existing cabinetry, such as building the wine cabinet (p. 80) to serve as a dedicated base cabinet that matches the style of your kitchen. You can sometimes borrow design elements from a nearby piece of furniture, such as a particular edging profile or door frame treatment. And you can personalize your pieces further by "signing" them with your own custom wood pulls or faux finish.

Allowing for future expansion

Don't forget to plan ahead, especially if you have collectors in the family. You may *think* you'll never own 100 CDs. Uh huh. Your wife may *promise* to cut back on buying new baking supplies. Right. Years ago, I vowed never to maintain more than one file cabinet's worth of paperwork. Well, I'm up to five now. (But that's it!) In any case, incorporate some extra space from the start, but don't overdo it. You can usually just build more units when they're needed, but it's surprising how quickly you can run out of room in the original piece.

Materials

All of the projects in this book are made from a combination of solid wood and hardwood plywood. A few of them involve a bit of simple veneer work. Most of the projects incorporate some hardware, ranging from screws and hinges to locks and pulls. None of the materials is hard to find.

Solid wood is available from lumber suppliers, mills, home-supply centers, and mail-order sources. Hardwood plywood can be purchased at some home-supply centers and wood dealers. You may also be able to buy it from a friendly commercial cabinet shop. Veneer is harder to find and often needs to be purchased by mail order. All of the hardware is available either at your local hardware store, at your local home-supply center, or through the mail-order suppliers listed in "Sources" (p. 172).

Solid wood

Wood is a beautiful material, but you have to understand a few things about its basic properties to work with it successfully. In solid form, it's a whole different animal than in its stable plywood form.

Solid wood moves. It always will, and you have to account for that fact or your project may self-destruct over time. If you restrain a solid-wood panel by gluing it into a frame, for example, the panel can crack or can explode the joints in the frame. If you glue a tabletop to its aprons, the top will almost

Fastening a Tabletop

Tabletop clips allow a solid-wood tabletop to move across the width of the grain.

Tabletop

Apron

Panel moves across the grain.

Tabletop clip

Tabletop

Apron

Set clip back from side apron to allow for expansion.

certainly crack over time. If you don't allow enough room for movement in a drawer front, it can swell and stick in its frame, causing possible damage to the pull when someone tugs heartily on it to open the drawer. But don't be discouraged, if you remember just a few rules of thumb, your projects will probably outlive you.

First, remember that wood expands and contracts *across* the grain. Movement *along* the grain is negligible and not really a concern in most furniture. What this means is that you can fit a panel in a frame fairly tightly at its ends, but you need to allow room at the sides. How much room depends on the season during which you're building

Stability Is in the Cut

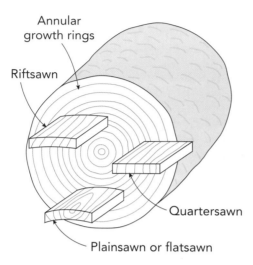

Annular growth rings

Riftsawn

Quartersawn

Plainsawn or flatsawn

The section of the log from which a board is cut largely determines how much it will shrink and warp. Quartersawn boards—evidenced by annular rings that run perpendicular to the face of the board—are the most stable. Riftsawn boards are moderately stable, whereas plainsawn boards are most prone to seasonal expansion and contraction, as well as warp.

(see "Fitting Solid-Wood Panels," p. 155). When attaching a solid-wood tabletop to an apron, as in the kitchen work station (p. 94), use tabletop clips that screw to the panel and insert into slots in the apron. Set the clips back from the side aprons a bit to allow the top to expand. When fitting solid-wood drawers, consider the season during which you're building. If working during the humid summer months, fit the drawers fairly snug in their openings. Come the dry winter months, they'll shrink a bit without leaving too big and unsightly a gap.

Of course, wood doesn't just move across the grain. It can also warp in many ways—cupping, bowing, and twisting. You can minimize warp by using properly dried lumber and letting it acclimate to your shop for at least a few days before cutting into it. Sometimes, you really need a stable piece of solid wood because you don't have any way of restraining it within a frame, such as with

the compartment door in the medicine cabinet (p. 158). In that case, use quartersawn wood, which is simply a piece of wood that has been cut from the log so that the annular rings run perpendicular to the face of the board. The next best cut is riftsawn. Try to avoid using plainsawn lumber for unrestrained panels.

Hardwood plywood

Plywood has certain advantages over solid wood, the primary one being that it is stable, so you don't have to worry about accommodating wood movement. You can fit plywood panels snugly into frames or drawer side grooves without worry. Because of its stability, it's ideal for panels that must fit tightly between legs, such as the platform on the kitchen work station (p. 94). Hardwood plywood also makes a great substrate for veneering.

Hardwood plywood isn't cheap; but, on a square foot basis, it's typically less expensive than solid wood. Stay away from construction plywood, particularly as a veneer substrate. It's often full of voids and prone to warpage and delamination.

Hardwood plywood does have its disadvantages, of course. Because the face veneer is so thin, it's subject to damage that's not easy to repair. Also, whenever the panel edges will be exposed, they'll need to be covered with solid wood. Alternatively, you can cover the edges with commercial veneer tape, but I generally shy away from veneer tape because of potential delamination problems. I've seen it happen too often.

Veneer

Veneer provides the opportunity to really dress up a project relatively inexpensively. In fact, many fancy woods are available only in veneer form these days. Plus, some cuts—such as the burl veneer on the man's jewelry box (p. 118)—would be troublesome to use in solid-wood form because of potential warpage problems. Veneering also allows you to match an exposed back panel to its case wood without having to buy an entire piece of expensive hardwood plywood.

That's why I used it on the back panel for the audiocassette cabinet (p. 32).

To those who haven't tried it, veneering may seem daunting. However, the simple veneering you'll find in this book, isn't difficult at all. Just follow the step-by-step instructions, and you'll be amazed that you ever thought it was hard to do. One caveat: Don't use contact cement for veneering. It may be the easiest way to attach the veneer, but most experienced woodworkers have learned not to trust the longevity of the bond.

Veneer is available from many mail-order suppliers, a few of which are listed in "Sources" (p. 172).

Hardware

Hinges, pulls, catches, drawer slides, locks, screws, and other hardware are essential parts of many projects. They contribute not only to the proper operation of doors, drawers, and lids but to the overall personality of the piece. There is a universe of different hardware out there, and you have a lot of options when it comes its design, quality, and cost. I recommend, though, that you don't skimp in this area. After putting all that work into constructing a fine piece, why sully it with cheap, poorly made hardware?

The sad truth is, it's difficult to find good hardware at your local hardware store or home-supply center. To get good-quality extruded hinges, brass ball catches, cupboard locks, and the like, you'll probably need to purchase them by mail order. Check "Sources" (p. 172) for a list of suppliers. In the cut list for every project, I've also listed a supplier and part number for the specific hardware used.

Perhaps the most ubiquitous hardware found in cabinetry is the common screw. Common as they are, screws are often installed incorrectly. One typical mistake is not drilling a shank clearance hole for a screw when fastening two workpieces together. The clearance hole, drilled in the "upper" workpiece, allows the screw to pass freely though it, drawing the two pieces fully

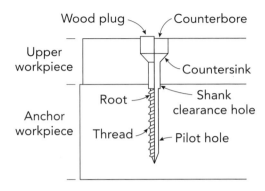

Installing a Screw

To fasten workpieces with a screw, a shank clearance hole in the upper piece allows the screw to draw the two boards fully together. A pilot hole allows the screw threads to penetrate the wood without having the screw head snap off. Flat-head screws need to be countersunk, and wood plugs require a counterbore.

together. In addition, a pilot hole often needs to be drilled to allow the screw threads to penetrate the wood without having the screw head snap off. In softwoods, the pilot hole should match the diameter of the screw's root. In hardwoods, the pilot hole should be slightly less than the thread diameter.

If installing a flat-head screw, you'll need to countersink the workpiece to accept the tapered bottom of the screw head. Many types of countersinks are available, some of which incorporate a pilot bit for quicker work. If you're going to hide the screws with plugs, as in the printer stand (p. 54), you'll need to drill counterbores to accept the plugs.

Small brass screws are often used for installing brass hinges, catches, and other hardware. Always drill a pilot hole to prevent the soft brass heads from snapping off. It's also wise to pre-thread the pilot hole using a steel screw of the same size as the brass screw. If you want to lubricate a screw

Shelf supports come in a wide variety of styles and materials.

Dado, Groove, and Rabbet Joints

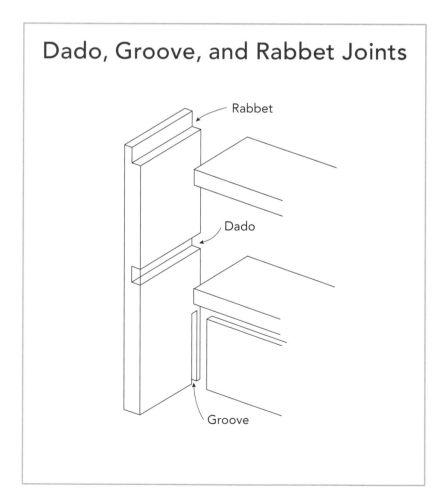

for easier driving, use wax. Don't use soap, as it attracts water and thus corrosion. Use a screwdriver that fits snugly into the screw slot without slop. I never power-drive small brass screws because they're so easy to snap.

Another type of hardware that's commonly used in these projects is the shelf support. You have a lot of choices here, so can pick whatever type you like.

Joinery

The joinery in these projects can all be done with common woodworking tools, as explained in the step-by-step text. You also have the option of altering the joinery to suit your particular tools. For example, if you don't own a biscuit joiner, you can often attach parts with dowels or splines instead. Sometimes you can use biscuits instead of tenons, but don't expect the same strength. Whatever joint you choose as a substitute, make sure it's appropriate for the application. Here's an overview of the joints used for the projects in this book.

Dado, groove, and rabbet joints

Dadoes, grooves, and rabbets are among the simplest of joints to make. One half of each joint is simply the squarely cut edge of one of the workpieces. In the case of dadoes and grooves, the edge is housed between two shoulders on the mating piece. With a rabbet joint, the workpiece sits against a single shoulder. The only difference between a dado and a groove is that a dado runs cross-grain whereas a groove runs with the grain.

Dado joints are often used to join shelves and dividers to case sides, tops, and bottoms. One of the most common uses for grooves is to hold a drawer bottom in place. Rabbets are frequently used to house case backs.

Rabbet-and-dado joint

One common joint is the rabbet-and-dado joint, which is often used to attach pieces at right angles, such as in case and drawer corners. But it can also be used to join shelves to case sides, because it's a little simpler than cutting tenons on the ends of the shelves. This is a fairly strong joint if fit and glued properly. When using it to join shelves to case sides, orient the tongue downward for better strength.

Mortise-and-tenon joints

The mortise-and-tenon joint is a time-honored method of joining pieces of wood at an angle. The joint is very strong and reliable. Although you can cut tenons with a handsaw and then drill and chop the mortises, the quickest way to make the joint is with machines. Tenons are typically cut on the table saw, as described in the step-by-step project instructions, and the mortises are routed out. The mortises are always cut first, and the tenons are sawn to fit them.

A perfectly viable alternative to the traditional mortise-and-tenon joint is the loose, or "floating," tenon joint. Rather than incorporating the tenon as an integral part of one of the workpieces, the joint consists of two mating mortises that accept an independent tenon. Loose tenon joinery is used in the file cabinet project (p. 68).

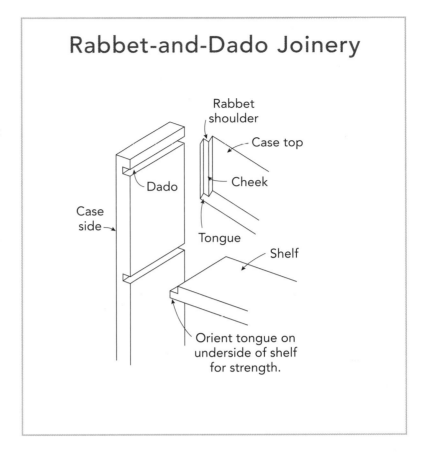

Rabbet-and-Dado Joinery

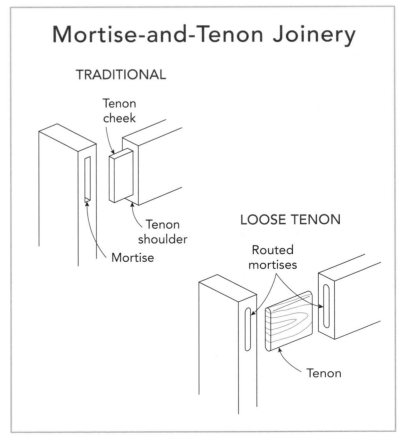

Mortise-and-Tenon Joinery

Biscuit Joinery

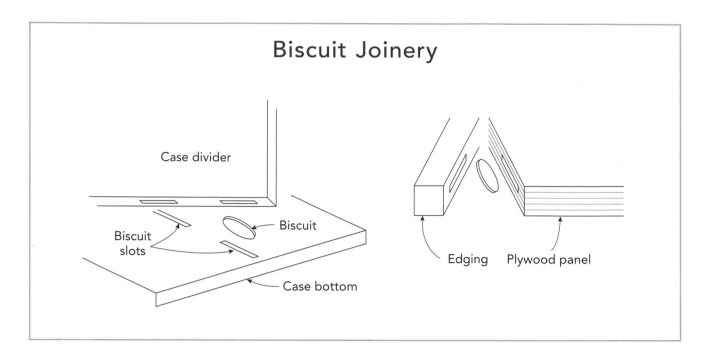

Case divider

Biscuit slots

Biscuit

Case bottom

Edging   Plywood panel

Biscuit joints

A relatively new development in joinery, the biscuit, or "plate," joint employs compressed, laminated, football-shaped splines that are glued into mating slots in the workpieces. Biscuits make for fairly strong joints and allow some lateral movement for aligning the workpieces. The compressed wood biscuits swell in their slots after glue is applied. Biscuits are a particularly convenient way to join case pieces at right angles, as you'll find in the desktop organizer (p. 42) and kitchen work station (p. 94) projects. This joint also aligns and attaches edging and miter joints, as seen in the man's jewelry box (p. 118).

Spline joints

If you don't own a biscuit joiner or if you want absolute maximum strength and alignment all along the joint, you can use spline joinery. I'm particularly fond of using splines to join case miters, as used in the

Spline Joinery

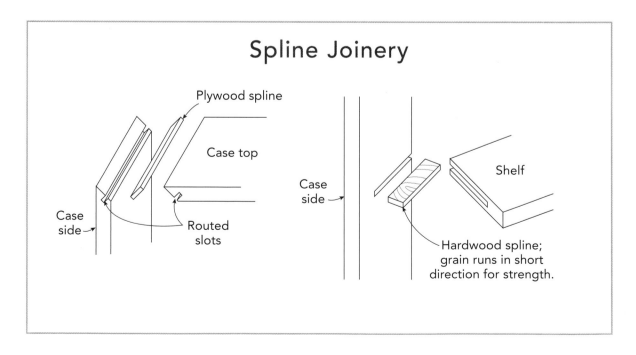

Plywood spline

Case top

Case side

Routed slots

Case side

Shelf

Hardwood spline; grain runs in short direction for strength.

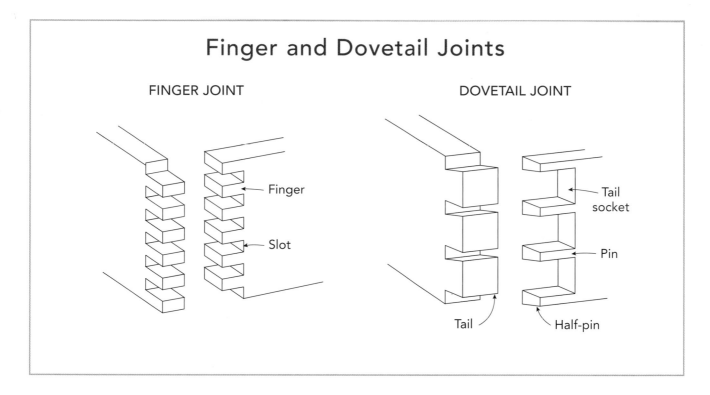

Finger and Dovetail Joints

FINGER JOINT

Finger

Slot

DOVETAIL JOINT

Tail socket

Pin

Tail

Half-pin

audiocassette cabinet (p. 32) and wine cabinet (p. 80). To make the joint, you simply rout identical grooves in the mating pieces and then glue a wooden spline into them.

Finger joints and dovetails

Finger joints and dovetails are two of the strongest methods for attaching workpieces at an angle. Finger joints, also called box joints, are most often used to connect drawer corners. Dovetails are also commonly used for drawer joinery but are seen joining case sides to case tops and bottoms, too. Finger joints are easy to make on the table saw, as explained in the directions for the desktop organizer (p. 42). Dovetails are easy to make using one of the many commercial jigs available. But you can also cut them by hand, as shown in the bed pedestal (p. 108). If you've got only a drawer or two to dovetail, you can often cut them by hand quicker than you can set up a jig.

Tools

All of the projects in this book were built using a basic complement of small-shop tools and equipment. In this section, we'll take a look at some of them and discuss alternative ways to go about a technique if you're lacking certain tools or machines.

Layout tools

Good work depends on accurate layout and measurement. You don't need an awful lot of layout tools, but the ones you have should be accurate and useful. You need at least a few squares of different sizes, a ruler and tape measure, a marking gauge, a bevel gauge, a sharp marking knife, and an awl. If you're buying layout tools, don't skimp on the quality. You can't cut correctly unless you can mark and measure correctly. For example, get a good steel rafter square instead of a framing square, as the former is often better made and more accurate.

Cutting tools

Among the cutting tools that you'll need are good drill bits, sawblades, and router bits. Woodworking requires a lot of drilling, so

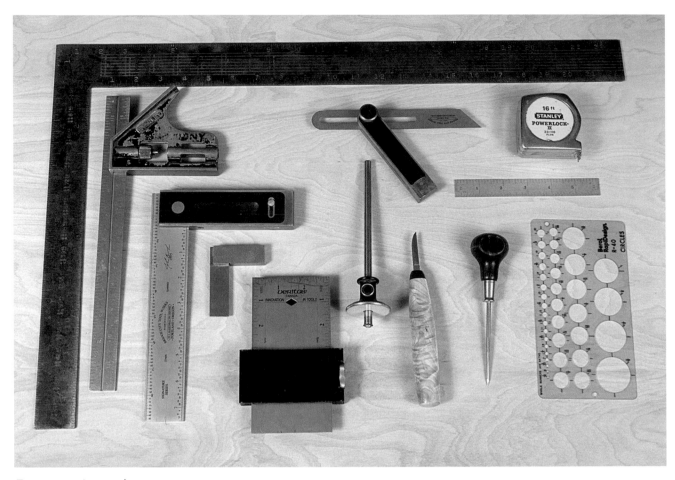

For measuring and marking, you need a basic complement of accurate tools. *From left:* rafter square, combination square, large and small try squares, "sliding" square, bevel gauge, marking gauge, tape measure, marking knife, 6-in. ruler, awl, and circle template.

use good bits. Standard twist drills are actually designed for cutting metal. For woodworking, you want bits that will neatly shear the wood fibers as they cut, so use the right tools for the job.

Good-quality circular sawblades are also important because the majority of the workpieces are cut on the table saw. I use a high-quality carbide combination blade that does the work of both ripping and crosscutting with very little tearout, even in plywood. I paid nearly $100 for it, but it's worth every penny. Good-quality dado heads are even more expensive, but necessary for cleanly cut dadoes, rabbets, tenons, and grooves. When it comes to sawblades, you generally get what you pay for. Check tool reviews in woodworking magazines and online message boards to get suggestions for good blades. I've listed a couple of suppliers in "Sources" (p. 172).

You'll also need a few good router bits, including a couple of straight or spiral bits

for cutting mortises, a flush-trimming bit for routing edging, and a slot-cutting bit for routing grooves. If you don't already have these bits, they'll be a great addition to your arsenal. Buy carbide bits; steel bits burn out far too quickly to be worth the initial cost savings.

As for hand tools for cutting, you probably already have a set of chisels and a few handplanes. Just make sure they're good and sharp for use. One other tool I highly recommend is a cabinet scraper. Basically just a steel card with a turned edge, it's hard to beat a scraper when it comes to smoothing wood. There's plenty of information to be found in magazines and books on the subjects of sharpening chisels, planes, and scrapers.

Equipment and accessories

Depending on the projects you want to make, you'll need some basic woodworking equipment. The machines used include a

Standard twist drills (far left) were designed for drilling metal, not wood. Instead use bits designed to shear the wood fibers as they drill. *From right:* multi-spur bit, Forstner bit, spade bit with shearing tips, brad-point bit.

A good dado head will cleanly cut a variety of joints. To set up this stack dado, mount the appropriate width chippers between the two outer blades, shimming between the chippers and blades to fine-tune the width of the dado head for a specific cut.

A crosscut sled is invaluable for cutting panels as well as for general crosscutting purposes. Its long fence and double runners make it much more accurate than a standard miter gauge, particularly for cutting 90-degree angles. For cutting miters, you can screw a temporary fence to the sled panel.

table saw, jointer, thickness planer, drill press, bandsaw, lathe, and biscuit joiner as well as, of course, a router or two. It would be hard to get by without a table saw, but you could probably find alternatives to the other machines.

If you don't have a jointer or thickness planer, you could use handplanes. You could use a hand drill instead of a drill press. If you don't have a bandsaw, you may be able to get by with a jigsaw for scroll work, or by thickness planing stock instead of resawing it. No lathe? Borrow time on a friend's, or ask him to do the turning. If you don't have a biscuit joiner, you could use dowels or splines instead. If you don't have a router (imagine *that*!), you could drill and chop mortises by hand.

Helpful accessories to have on hand include a good router edge guide and a crosscut sled for the table saw.

General Tips and Techniques

For each project, I've provided step-by-step instructions particular to that piece. Here, I'll discuss certain general woodworking procedures that apply to just about every project you make.

Laying out and stock preparation

Reading cut lists The dimensions in the cut lists are presented in order of thickness, then width, and finally length. Note that the length dimension always follows the grain direction of lumber or the face grain of plywood. Although finished sizes are given in the cut list, it's best to take your workpiece measurement directly from an opening or frame when appropriate, such as when fitting backs, drawer bottoms, or inset doors and drawer fronts.

Laying out Along with the actual shape of a project, the grain patterns on the individual pieces largely determine the beauty of the finished furniture. Haphazard grain lines can ruin an otherwise graceful design. It's best to use straight grain for rails, aprons, stiles, legs, and other narrow frame members. Save the wilder grain for the center of door and case panels and for drawer fronts. If you have a run of side-by-side drawers, cut the drawer fronts from the same board, maintaining the same grain continuity on the finished piece. Composing with grain when laying out large panels is discussed in more detail on p. 99.

For tips on dressing lumber after laying it out, see p. 36. It's usually wise to mill extra stock for tool setups at the same time you mill your project stock. That way, you can be assured the test pieces will be the same dimensions as the project stock.

When laying out plywood, I always inspect it first for flaws using a strong, glancing sidelight in a darkened shop (see the photos on p. 133). I sweep the light both

Translating Cut Lists

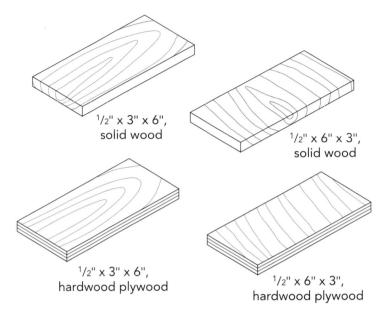

1/2" x 3" x 6", solid wood

1/2" x 6" x 3", solid wood

1/2" x 3" x 6", hardwood plywood

1/2" x 6" x 3", hardwood plywood

Cut list dimensions are listed in order of thickness, then width, and then length. The length dimension always follows the grain direction of lumber or the face grain of plywood. Although the pieces shown here are all the same size, their cut list dimensions are listed differently.

Grain Layout

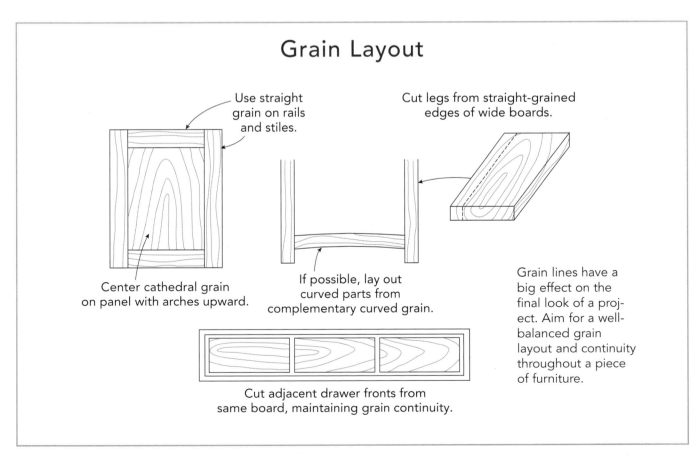

Use straight grain on rails and stiles.

Cut legs from straight-grained edges of wide boards.

Center cathedral grain on panel with arches upward.

If possible, lay out curved parts from complementary curved grain.

Grain lines have a big effect on the final look of a project. Aim for a well-balanced grain layout and continuity throughout a piece of furniture.

Cut adjacent drawer fronts from same board, maintaining grain continuity.

Triangle Marking System

Using triangles to orient your workpieces provides a quick reference for machining and assembly. As you can see here, a triangle immediately identifies the top, bottom, left side, and right side of an assembly.

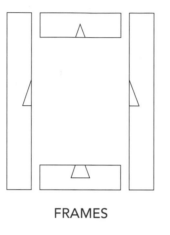

FRAMES

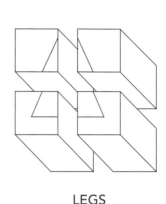

LEGS

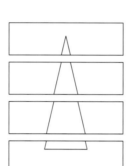

PANELS OR DRAWER FRONTS

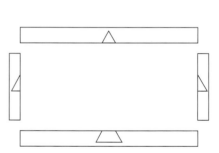

APRONS OR DRAWER BOXES

along and across the grain. Remember that plywood often varies in thickness from piece to piece. Thus dado joints and rabbet joints will fit better if all of the parts that slip into those joints are cut from the same piece of plywood.

For orienting individual parts, I use the triangle marking system, which tells me at a glance how a part relates to its mates.

Assembly tips

✦ I typically apply glue to both mating surfaces, except when applying edging. For that, I apply a thick coat just to the plywood edge. An ink roller works well for spreading a thin, even coat of glue.

For brushing glue onto tenons, tongues, and into mortises, I use a solder flux brush. A small artists brush is good for getting into small holes and grooves.

✦ When gluing up, work on a flat surface. If a piece isn't lying flat, you won't be able to check it accurately for square.

✦ Use contact cement to attach thick leather pads to pipe clamp jaws, preventing damage to workpieces.

✦ Use cauls to distribute clamping pressure, centering them over the joint. To span long joints, use crowned cauls. On smaller pieces, it's easier to use cauls that almost cover the entire piece being clamped.

- If a piece isn't square under clamping pressure, try shifting the angle of the clamps on the joints to bring it into square.
- Always do a dry clamp-up to rehearse your clamping procedure. While a cabinet is dry-clamped, fit its back snugly into its rabbets so you'll be able to insert it unglued to hold the case square while the glue cures.
- To clean up excess glue, use a clean rag and clean water, replenishing the water as necessary to prevent wiping diluted glue into wood grain and jeopardizing the finish. Alternatively, wait until the glue has cured to a rubbery consistency and then pare it away with a very sharp chisel.

A favorite finish

I've used a lot of different finishes over the years, including tung oil, various Danish oils, homemade oil-and-varnish mixes, nitrocellulose lacquer, and polyurethane. There's one finish that I'm particularly fond of that yields a beautiful, soft luster without a thick build sitting on top of the workpiece. It's a mixture of oil and varnish that's heavy on the latter and is called a "wiping varnish" by some finishing experts. It is resistant to water, alcohol, and abrasion and is easy to repair. The smooth, soft, luster is largely a result of the method of application, which I'll describe here. Several manufacturers make a version of this finish, which is sometimes sold under the names "tung oil finish" and "Danish oil finish."

Begin by sanding the surfaces through 220-grit; then thoroughly brush off the sanding dust. Check for glue splotches by inspecting the pieces under a strong side-light in a darkened shop or by wiping suspect surfaces with mineral spirits or naphtha. It's a good idea to prepare your finish rags ahead of time: Tear cotton sheeting into pieces about 20-in. square.

The product I use comes in two different mixes: a sealer and a top coat (see "Sources"

Clamping Cauls

Cauls distribute clamping pressure across joints. Make long cauls from thick hardwood. Cutting the ends squarely will aid in assembly when standing the cauls on end on the bench.

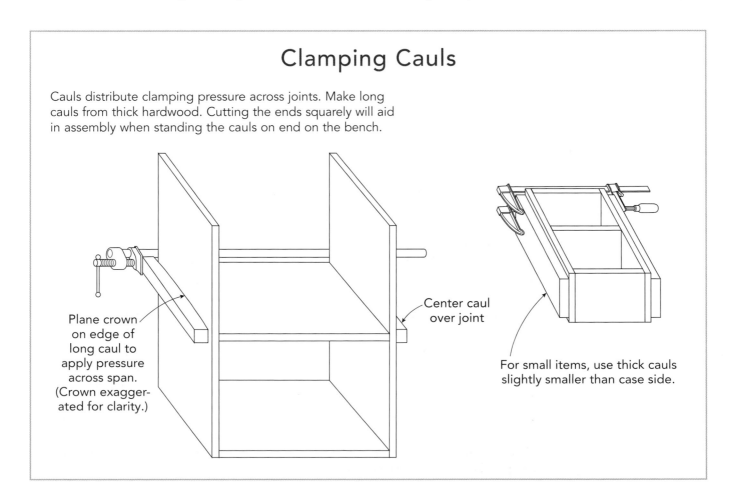

Plane crown on edge of long caul to apply pressure across span. (Crown exaggerated for clarity.)

Center caul over joint

For small items, use thick cauls slightly smaller than case side.

Flood the initial sealer coat onto the workpieces. For absorbent woods, the author uses a brush. For most hardwoods, application with a rag is more efficient and wastes less finish.

on p. 172). The sealer mixture is relatively thin and soaks well into the wood. Use it for the first coat. On absorbent woods, use a brush to flood the sealer into the wood, because it soaks up so quickly. On harder woods, use a rag, applying it more sparingly so as not to waste a lot of finish when wiping off the excess. Use a small artist's brush to work the finish into shelf support holes or small notches. Let the sealer coat soak in and apply more finish to "dry" spots as needed. Some softwoods seem to never quit soaking in the finish. No matter. Just make sure you get a lot of finish into the wood. When the wood no longer seems hungry, wipe off the excess finish thoroughly and let it dry overnight.

The next day, sand the finished wood fairly vigorously with 400-grit wet/dry sili-con carbide paper, lubricating the paper and the surface with mineral spirits. Wipe off the excess spirits afterward.

Next, apply the second coat of finish, using the top coat mixture. This is thicker than the sealer and sets up tack more quickly, so you'll need to work smaller areas at a time. To put on this coat, and all subsequent top coats, use a rag formed into a "bob" by crumpling the edges of the rag backward into the center to create a small bag. Lightly dip the face of the bob into the finish and wipe it onto the workpiece. (Avoid soaking the rag, as you'll be using it to wipe off the excess finish.) Repeat this application procedure until you've covered an area the size of which you'll be able to handle before the finish tacks up too much. Experiment by working fairly small areas for starters.

When the finish starts to tack up, which is pretty quickly with this top coat, start wiping off the excess. Use the same rag, undoing the bob and crumpling the rag to disperse the residual finish throughout. Wipe the surface thoroughly, rubbing it vigorously and quickly. If the finish becomes too tacky to wipe, simply apply fresh finish to soften it. As you wipe, the rag should become about as tacky as a commercial tack cloth used to remove dust. Perfect. This will leave a very thin coat of finish on the surface. When the rag becomes wet, replace it with a fresh one. Avoid soft cloths, such as old T-shirts, because they're too absorbent. When you've coated all the surfaces, let the work dry overnight.

For the third coat, begin by wet sanding with 600-grit wet/dry sandpaper. Then repeat the above procedures. You'll find that every new top coat dries more quickly and leaves the work a bit shinier. After the third coat dries, dry scrub it with 0000 steel wool, carefully brushing off the residue and blowing off the workpieces with compressed air.

Wipe on one last coat in the same manner as before. I find that these four coats are usually sufficient to impart a wonderful luster to the project, but I'll generally apply one more coat to tabletops and other surfaces that can expect more than their fair share of liquids and abrasion.

> ### WARNING
> ✦ ✦ ✦
> When finishing, work in a well-ventilated area and dispose of rags properly. To prevent the spontaneous combustion of the rags, lay or hang them out flat to dry or submerge them in water.

Apply the top coats using a rag formed into a "bob": Crumple the edges of the rag backward into the center.

MODULAR COMPACT DISC CABINET

COMPACT DISCS have become almost as common as books these days. Music CDs have largely replaced vinyl records, and you'll usually find a stack of computer program CDs within reach of any computer. While CDs can be stored almost anywhere, there are few spaces ideally suited to them. Placed on a typical bookshelf, they waste a lot of space. Stored in a drawer, they'll scatter unless restrained within compartments. Commercial storage units for CDs are often unattractive, poorly made, and ill-suited to the size of your particular collection. A large unit may sit mostly empty for a long time, but a small unit can fill up more quickly than you'd think.

To solve those problems, I designed these cabinets as individual boxes, or modules, that are screwed together. A modular cabinet can be built to suit your current collection, but can be easily expanded to accommodate future discs when needed. The walnut cabinet shown here is composed of three modules stacked vertically, but you can configure the boxes any way you like. The modules are visually tied together by sandwiching them between top and bottom "caps," creating the look of a finished cabinet. As your CD collection grows, you can simply unscrew a cap, add a module, then re-attach the cap. If you like, you can hang the cabinets on a wall by screwing through the plywood back into wall studs.

MODULAR COMPACT DISC CABINET

Like barrister bookcases, these CD modules are stacked together to create the look of a single cabinet. The modules are screwed together and sandwiched between top and bottom caps.

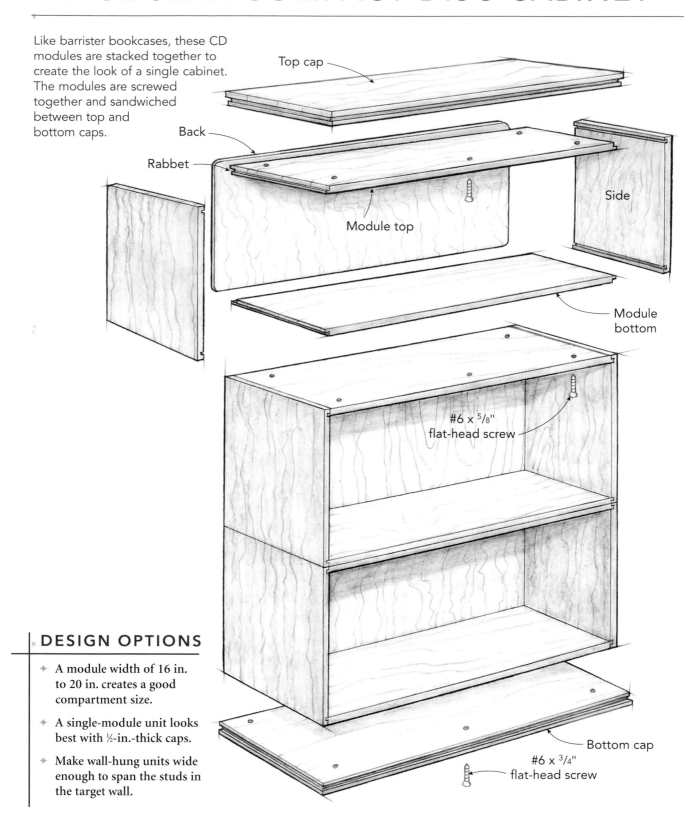

Top cap

Back

Rabbet

Module top

Side

Module bottom

#6 x $^{5}/_{8}$"
flat-head screw

Bottom cap

#6 x $^{3}/_{4}$"
flat-head screw

DESIGN OPTIONS

◆ A module width of 16 in. to 20 in. creates a good compartment size.

◆ A single-module unit looks best with ½-in.-thick caps.

◆ Make wall-hung units wide enough to span the studs in the target wall.

Cabinet Modules

To expand the cabinet vertically, remove a cap, add a module, and re-attach the cap. To expand the cabinet horizontally, make new top and bottom caps for the new modules.

SINGLE-MODULE CABINET

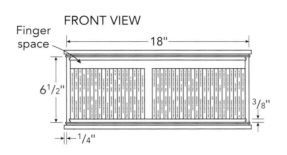

FRONT VIEW

Finger space

18"

6½"

3/8"

¼"

SIDE VIEW

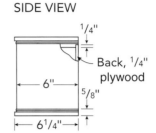

¼"

Back, ¼" plywood

6"

5/8"

6¼"

THREE-MODULE CABINET

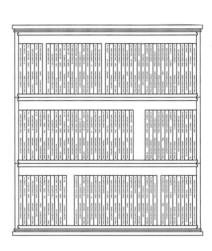

FOUR-MODULE CABINET

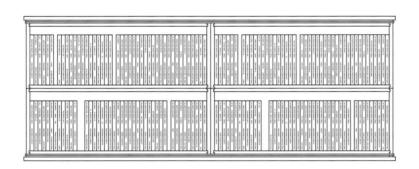

THE CABINET MODULES use simple rabbet-and-dado joint construction with a plywood back The top and bottom caps provide a lot of the appeal and are simply attached to the modules, tying them together visually.

Milling and Shaping the Stock

Lay out and prepare the stock

You could plane the ⅜-in.-thick stock down from store-bought ¾-in.-thick lumber, but it's much less wasteful to resaw the pieces from thick roughsawn stock. You'll get the best yield by using 6/4 or thicker stock, but

CUT LIST FOR COMPACT DISC CABINET

6	Sides	⅜" x 6" x 6½"	solid wood
6	Box tops/ bottoms	⅜" x 6" x 17½"	solid wood
2	Caps	⅝" x 6¼" x 18½"	solid wood
3	Backs	¼" x 6¼" x 17¾"	hardwood plywood

Other materials

15	#6 x ⅝" flat-head wood screws
5	#6 x ¾" flat-head wood screws

Dimensions for an 18"-wide, three-module unit.

RESAWING ON THE BANDSAW

Resawing is a great way to economize on lumber when making thin pieces. But to do it successfully, your saw needs to be tuned properly and the fence needs to be set to accommodate "blade drift"—the blade's tendency to pull to one side.

Here are a few tips:

+ Use the widest blade your saw will accept and tension it so there is no more than ¼-in. flex with the blade guides set at maximum height. New blades cut and track the best.

+ Set the thrust bearings just a few thousandths of an inch behind the blade.

+ Set the guide blocks a few thousands of an inch (the thickness of a dollar bill) to the sides of the blade and just behind the tooth gullets.

+ Make a tall, flat, straight fence and set it to the angle of your blade drift. Make sure the blade and fence are parallel to each other.

+ Saw using a steady, even feed pressure, holding the workpiece firmly against the fence just in front of the blade, as shown at left. Pull the last inch or so through from the outfeed side of the saw.

+ Before making each subsequent slice from a workpiece, joint the face that will abut the fence.

if you're careful you can even saw two ⅜-in.-thick pieces from roughsawn 4/4 stock.

1. Lay out the pieces, allowing a couple of inches extra in length. Gang the side pieces together end to end to make for safer jointing and planing and to provide grain continuity on the cabinet sides, if desired. Lay out some extra stock for tool setup purposes and to allow for mistakes.

2. Cut the tops, bottoms, and caps to rough length, but keep the ganged sides together as a continuous piece for right now.

3. Joint one edge of each piece straight, rip it about ¼-in. oversize in width, then joint one face flat.

4. Resaw the pieces, then plane them to finished thickness (see "Resawing on the Bandsaw").

5. Joint one edge of each piece straight and square, rip the pieces to final width, and crosscut one end of each piece square.

6. Draw a line across the side pieces to register their relationships to each other, then crosscut all pieces to finished length. Use a stop block to ensure consistency of length.

Saw the joints and cap edging

1. Determine the inside face of each piece, then sand all the inside faces to 220-grit, being careful not to round over the edges.

2. Saw the ⅛-in. by ⅛-in. dadoes in the side pieces (see "Details"). Space the dadoes in from the ends so that the sides will overhang the top and bottom by about ¹⁄₆₄ in. To create a relatively flat-bottom dado, use a sawblade that includes raker teeth (see **photo A**).

3. Using scrap, set up your saw to cut the ⅛-in. by ¼-in. rabbets in the tops and bottoms. Cut the tongue to thickness first, making the test cut a bit fat. Remove the rabbet waste using a different saw so that you can leave your table saw set up as is. Next, test-fit the tongue in a dado. Adjust the saw fence until the tongue fits snugly, but not too tightly, then cut the tongues on all of the pieces (see **photo B** on p. 28).

4. Saw the rabbet shoulders (see **photo C** on p. 28). Again, use scrap for the initial setup.

5. With the raker-tooth blade on your saw, rip the profile in the front and side edges of the caps.

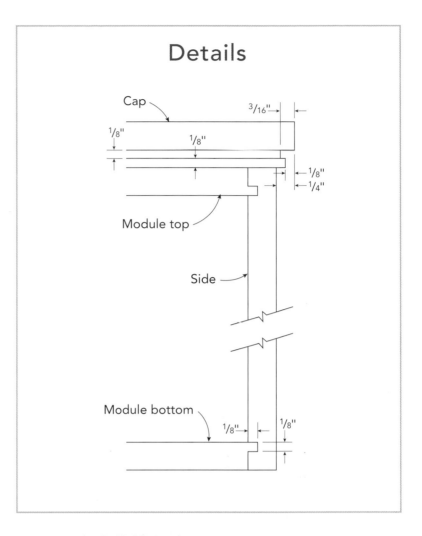

Details

Cap

3/16"

1/8"

1/8"

1/8"

1/4"

Module top

Side

Module bottom

1/8"

1/8"

PHOTO A: Press the stock firmly against the saw table to ensure dadoes of consistent depth.

PHOTO B: To make the rabbets on the box tops and bottoms, first cut each tongue to thickness, sliding it firmly against the table-saw rip fence.

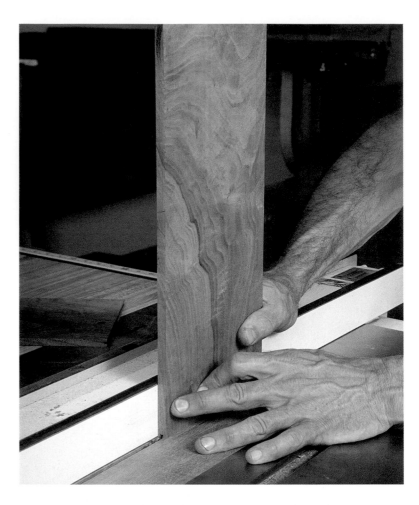

PHOTO C: Cut the shoulder of the rabbet using a board clamped to the rip fence above the rabbet to prevent the cutoff from jamming between the blade and fence.

PHOTO D: Place thick hardwood cauls against the box sides to distribute clamping pressure along the joints.

Assembling the Case

Assemble and rout the modules

1. Mark all the pieces for their final position, remembering to pair up the sides to ensure continuous grain, if desired. I use the triangle marking system, shown on p. 18, to orient the pieces.

2. Glue up each module using thick cauls against the sides to distribute clamping pressure across the joints (see **photo D**). After clamping, check for square by comparing the diagonal measurements. If necessary, cock the clamps to bring the unit into square.

3. After the glue has cured, plane the edges of each module. Also plane the ends of the sides flush to the tops and bottoms.

4. Rout the ¼-in. by ¼-in. rabbet in the back edges of each module to accept a plywood back. Use a bit with a small bearing that can reach well into the corner. An auxiliary router base will stabilize the router on the thin workpiece edge (see **photo E**).

PHOTO E: To prevent tearout on the interior rabbet shoulder, first make a shallow "climb cut," carefully moving the router in a counterclockwise direction. Finish up by routing in a clockwise direction, as shown here.

SETTING THE DRIFT ANGLE

Any given bandsaw blade tends to cut in a particular direction, which isn't necessarily parallel to the edges of the saw table. To resaw successfully, your fence must be set to the angle the blade wants to cut.

1. Gauge a line parallel to the straight edge of a piece of scrap about 20 in. long (see top photo at left).

2. Carefully cut freehand to the line, stopping about halfway through the cut. Without changing the feed angle, hold the scrap firmly to the table and turn the saw off.

3. Trace the straight edge of the scrap onto the bandsaw table using a fine-tipped felt marker (see bottom photo at left).

4. Set the fence parallel to the line at a distance equal to the desired resaw thickness plus about $\frac{1}{32}$ in. and clamp it in place (see photo below).

5. Test the setup using scrap. The blade should track nicely without pulling the workpiece into or away from the fence. Adjust the fence as necessary to fine-tune the drift angle.

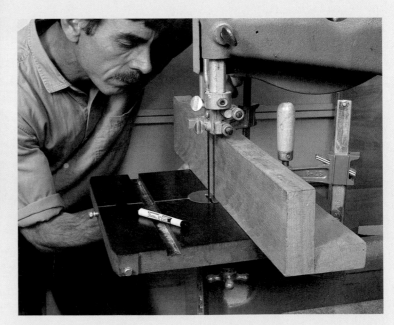

Attach the modules and caps

1. Clamp the top two modules and the top cap together upside down to the bench. Drill pilot holes and countersink holes for #6 by ⅝-in. flat-head screws (see **photo F**). If you don't have a right-angle drill, you can use a right-angle adapter (see **photo G**).

2. Unclamp the modules and enlarge the pilot holes in the countersunk pieces to allow the screw to slip through and draw the two pieces tightly together.

3. Clamp the bottom module and bottom cap to the center module and repeat the above processes. (I clamp the modules in steps because it's awkward to align and clamp a lot of pieces at once.) Counterbore for #6 by ¾-in. flat-head screws to attach the bottom cap.

4. Screw the modules together, leaving the caps off for now.

5. Touch-up sand the insides of the modules and sand or plane the outsides flush to each other.

6. Sand the caps and screw them to the modules.

Make the backs

1. Cut the backs for a tight fit within their rabbets. Then sand or saw the corners to match the radius of the rabbet corner.

2. If you're going to stain the backs to match the color of the modules, do it now. To preserve a perimeter of raw wood for gluing, lightly trace around the inside of the module onto the back, mask just outside of the lines, and then stain.

3. Use glue and nails or staples to fasten the backs. Even if you're not planning to hang the cabinets, it's wise to glue the backs anyway, in case someone decides to hang them later.

Finishing Up

You can use just about any finish you like on a CD cabinet because it's not likely to be subjected to liquids or abrasion. I typically use several coats of a wiping varnish on the ones I build (see "A Favorite Finish" on p. 19).

PHOTO F: Drill for the screw holes using a combination pilot/countersink bit. Afterward, enlarge the hole in the countersunk piece to allow the screw to pull the modules tightly together.

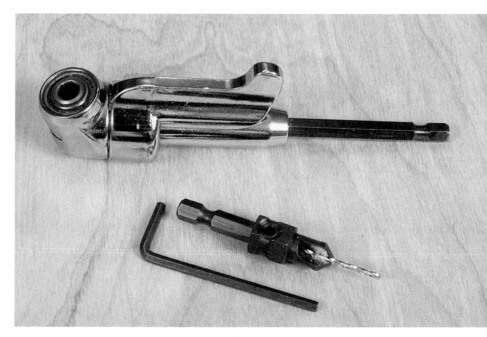

PHOTO G: A right-angle drill adapter is an inexpensive alternative to a right-angle drill. This particular adapter accepts hex shanks. Other types incorporate adjustable chucks.

AUDIOCASSETTE CABINET

AUDIOCASSETTE TAPES have been used for decades for music and voice recording and are likely to be around for a good while longer. In spite of the proliferation of recordable compact discs, cassettes still offer a good-quality, inexpensive recording format. Many contemporary music collections still exist on cassette tape and aren't likely to be thrown away soon.

An avid music collector myself, I've amassed hundreds of cassette tapes over the years. I've tried a variety of storage solutions for them, including drawers (which tend to strew tapes about) and stacked wine boxes (funky and ill-sized for the job.) For a while, I made cabinets that displayed the tapes horizontally. The titles were a bit easier to read that way, but the support spacers wasted valuable storage space. Also, when adding a new tape to an alphabetized collection, it was a pain to move every tape down one space.

Eventually, I arrived at the ideal solution. This cabinet, with its perfectly sized compartments, recessed shelves, and bottom riser block maximizes storage space and allows easy plucking of the tapes. Each tape projects ½ in. from the shelves, with ¾ in. clearance above and below for finger and thumb access. This particular mahogany case holds 140 tapes. Of course, you can size your case to suit the size of your own collection and available wall space. The splined miter corners create a clean look and very strong joint, with no end grain showing.

AUDIOCASSETTE CABINET

This cabinet holds 140 cassette tapes. The recessed shelves and riser and the extra space in the top section provide finger access for easy plucking from a full shelf.

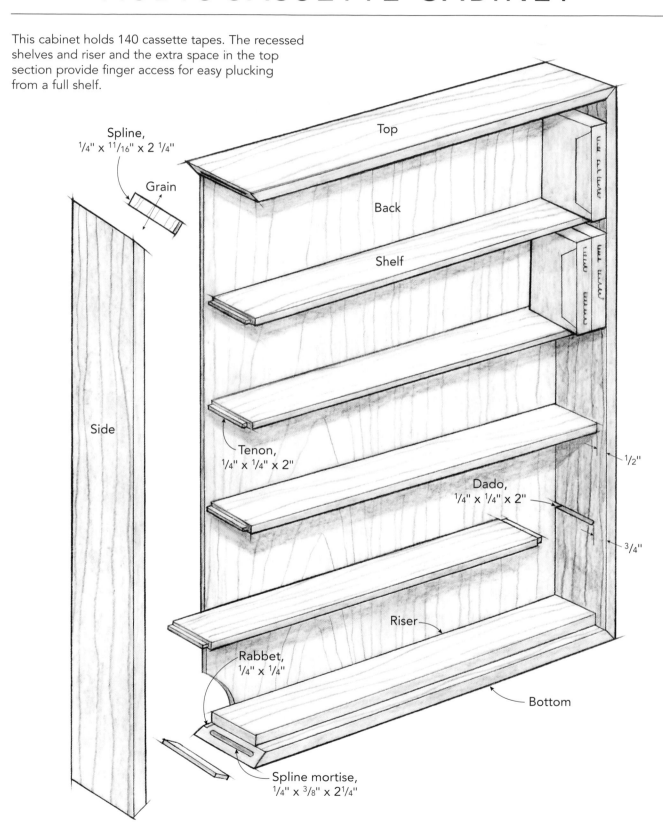

Spline,
1/4" x 11/16" x 2 1/4"

Grain

Top

Back

Shelf

Side

Tenon,
1/4" x 1/4" x 2"

Dado,
1/4" x 1/4" x 2"

1/2"

3/4"

Riser

Rabbet,
1/4" x 1/4"

Bottom

Spline mortise,
1/4" x 3/8" x 2 1/4"

Side and Front Views

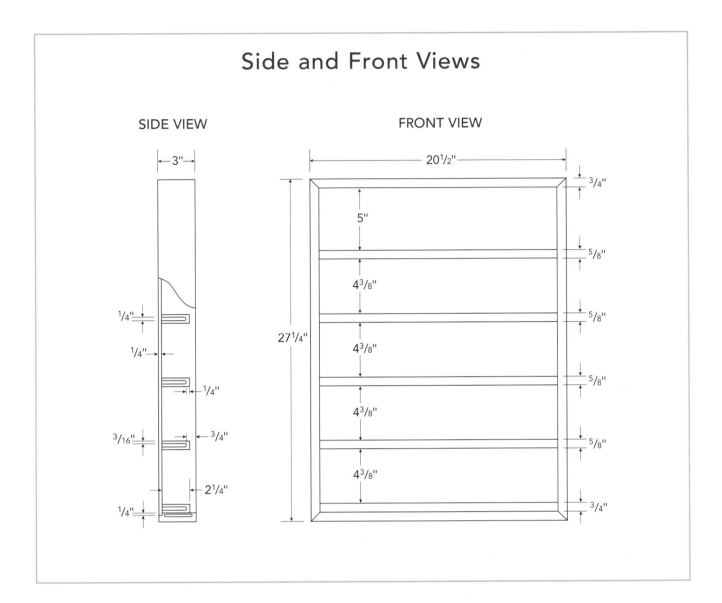

SIDE VIEW

FRONT VIEW

DESIGN OPTIONS

+ To customize the case width for a different number of tapes, stand the chosen number of tapes side by side and add ¼ in. for clearance.

+ Corner and shelf joints could be made using biscuits.

THIS SMALL OPEN CABINET uses splined miter joints at the four corners for simple construction and a clean look The spline grooves are cut with a plunge router after mitering the ends. To make these plunge cuts as easy as possible, the four sides are stacked together so there's a wider surface to work on.

Although the cabinet is simple to make, construction details, such as tenoned shelves and a rabbeted back, make it a sturdy piece that may well outlast the viability of the magnetic tape in the cassettes.

CUT LIST FOR AUDIOCASSETTE CABINET

2	Sides	¾" x 3" x 27¼"	solid wood
2	Top/bottom	¾" x 3" x 20½"	solid wood
4	Shelves	⅝" x 2¼" x 19½"	solid wood
1	Riser	¾" x 2¼" x 19"	solid wood
1	Back	¼" x 19½" x 26¼"	hardwood plywood
4	Splines	¼" x ¾" x 2¼"	solid wood

Other materials

Veneer	approx. 3' sq.	

Dimensions for all pieces with tenons include tenon length.

Making the Parts

Lay out and mill the parts

1. Lay out the pieces for the sides, top, bottom, shelves, and riser. Allow a couple of inches extra in length for all pieces. Include some extra stock for tool setup and possible mistakes. Don't cut the plywood back to size yet.

2. Plane the stock to thickness, rip the pieces to width, then crosscut to length. Make sure to dress the stock properly for straight, square pieces (see "Dressing Stock with Machines"). Leave the riser block just a bit long for right now.

3. Mark all of the pieces for orientation, using the triangle marking system described on p. 18.

DRESSING STOCK WITH MACHINES

To ensure accurate joinery and straight lines in your furniture, it's necessary to "dress" your stock flat, straight, and square. It's best to begin with oversize, roughsawn lumber, because it's already done most of its warping during the drying process. Therefore, you'll be able to plane and joint it to final thickness and width with minimal warping. If you begin with warped premilled lumber, you can't flatten it without losing thickness. Here's a quick overview of proper stock dressing using machinery. You can also flatten and thickness stock with handplanes following the same basic sequence.

1. If your roughsawn stock is fairly bowed or cupped, begin by ripping and crosscutting it into smaller pieces. For safe ripping on the table saw, joint one edge of the stock straight for feeding against the rip fence. Allow a couple extra inches in length and ¼ in. extra in width for each piece.

2. Flatten one face on the jointer. For stability, feed the stock with the concave face down. Cut with the slope of the grain to minimize tearout.

3. Plane the stock to final thickness, feeding it through a thickness planer, with the previously flattened side on the planer table. Cut with the slope of the grain.

4. Joint one edge of the thicknessed board square. Feed with the concave edge down.

5. Rip the piece to width on the table saw.

6. Crosscut one end square, measure for length, then crosscut the opposite end to length.

ROUTING SPLINE MITER MORTISES

To rout spline mortises in case miters, clamp the four case pieces together, as shown. This creates a square shoulder for the router fence and provides additional bearing for the router base. Carefully line up the tips of the miters; then clamp the boards as close to their ends as possible without obstructing router travel. Secure the clamped-up pieces in a vise or clamp them against the edge of a bench.

The router fence can be as simple as a straight piece of wood clamped to the router base. Adjust the fence so that the mortise favors the inside of the miter. Rout in the direction shown to prevent climb cutting. After routing the first two mortises on the inner pieces, slide the outer pieces to the opposite end, and rout the remaining mortises on the inner pieces. Then reverse the sandwich and rout the rest of the mortises in the same manner. This may seem a bit confusing at first, but once you've done it, you'll find it simple.

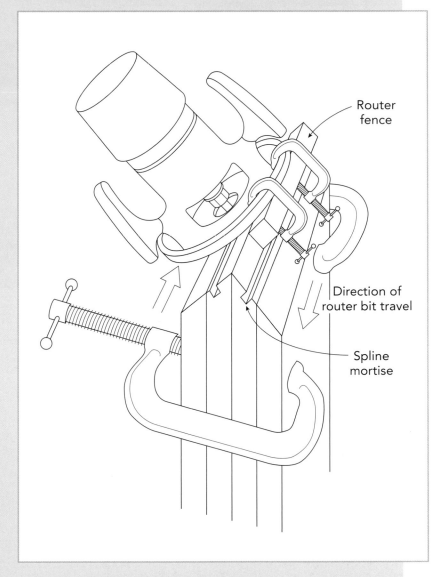

Router fence

Direction of router bit travel

Spline mortise

PHOTO A: A shopmade T-square clamped to the case side guides the router when cutting the shelf dadoes.

PHOTO B: To rout the spline mortises, first clamp the case walls together to form a peak. This creates a square shoulder for the router fence to ride against while providing sufficient bearing for the router base.

Cut the joints

1. Saw the miters on the ends of the sides, top, and bottom. Use a good-quality cross-cut blade on the table saw or sliding compound miter saw. Sand the inside faces of the sides, top, and bottom through 220 grit.

2. Lay out the shelf dadoes, stopping them ¾ in. from the front edge of each side (see "Side View" on p. 35). Remember to allow for the thickness of the riser and the ³⁄₁₆-in.-wide shoulders on the shelf tenons.

3. Rout the ¼-in.-deep shelf dadoes. I use a shopmade T-square to guide the router (see **photo A**).

4. Rip the ¼-in. by ¼-in. rabbet in the rear edges of the case sides, top, and bottom to accept the back panel.

5. Rout the ⅜-in.-deep spline mortises (see **photo B**). Space the mortises about ³⁄₁₆ in. away from the inside edge of the miter. Space them ¼ in. away from the front edge and ½ in. away from the rear edge. I clamp the case pieces together to create a square

corner for the router fence and to provide support for the router base (see "Routing Spline Miter Mortises" on p. 37).

6. Make the splines. For joint strength, orient the grain perpendicular to the miter joint line. The splines should fit the mortises snugly, but not too tightly. You should be able to push them in with only finger pressure. You can crosscut the splines from a strip of ¼-in. by 2¼-in. stock. Round the spline edges to match approximately the ends of the mortises.

7. Saw the tenons on the ends of the shelves. I use a dado head on the table saw, burying the unused part of the dado head under an auxiliary rip fence and using a miter gauge to guide the workpiece (see **photo C**). For the first cut, set the height of the blade for a fat tenon, then saw both cheeks. Raise the blade a bit and repeat, creeping up on the final cut until you have a snug fit in the dado.

PHOTO C: The shelf tenons can be cut using a dado head, an auxiliary saw fence, and a miter gauge. Center each tenon by making equal cuts from both sides. After cutting all of the long tenon shoulders, raise the blade ⅛ in. and cut all of the front shoulders.

PHOTO D:
Because the
entire case must
be glued up at
once, it's impor-
tant to do a dry
clamp-up first to
set your clamps
and rehearse your
procedures.

Miter Clamping Cauls

Cut chamfer after
gluing block to plywood.

Case

¼" plywood

Clamping miters can be tricky. Most commercial miter clamps
simply hold the pieces in contact; they don't apply pressure.
Band clamps apply pressure to only the outside edges of the
joint. A much better approach is to make miter clamping cauls,
which allow you to apply strong, positive pressure across the
entire joint.

8. Round over the front end of each tenon
with a chisel to match approximately the
radius at the front ends of the dadoes. Then
sand the shelves through 220 grit.

Assembling the Case

Clamp the case

1. Dry-fit the case together to make sure
everything fits well and to rehearse your
clamping procedures (see **photo D**). I use
miter clamping cauls to pull the corners
together (see "Miter Clamping Cauls").
Alternatively, you could use commercial
miter clamps or band clamps.

2. Apply glue to all of the joints at one side
of the case; then fit them together, making
sure that the outer case pieces are flush and
that the rear edges of the shelves are flush to
the back rabbet. Then, with the case standing on its assembled side, apply glue to the
remaining joints and attach the other side.
After clamping the assembly together,
immediately wipe off any excess glue with
clean water.

3. After the glue has dried, crosscut the riser block for a tight fit between the sides; then glue it to the case bottom.

Veneer and fit the back

For the back, I covered ¼-in.-thick hardwood plywood with mahogany veneer. Alternatively, you could use a complementary veneer or stain the back. For more on basic veneering, see the man's jewelry box on p. 118.

1. Cut a piece of ¼-in.-thick hardwood plywood for the back. Make it about ¼-in. oversize in length and width. Use a close-grained plywood, such as birch or maple.
2. Cut your veneer to the approximate size of the plywood. If it's necessary to edge join several pieces of veneer to make up the panel width, joint the mating edges first. To do this, sandwich the pieces of veneer between two pieces of thick stock. Lay the sandwich on the bench; then, using a sharp jack plane on its side, plane the edges of the slightly projecting veneer. Afterward, tape the pieces together on the "show" side of the veneer.
3. Glue the veneer to the plywood. I don't trust the longevity of contact cement, so I use yellow glue, applying an even coat to the plywood only. Press the veneer firmly into the glue using a hard roller or straight-sided jar.
4. Cover the face of the veneer with plastic wrap or waxed paper; then lay a thick plywood caul onto it. Weight the plywood down with cinderblocks or other heavy items until the glue cures.
5. Saw the plywood back for a tight fit into the case's rabbets, but don't install it yet.

Finishing Up

1. Sand the exterior of the case through 220 grit, making sure the miters meet nicely at the corners. Touch-up sand the shelves and other interior surfaces. Sand the back panel.

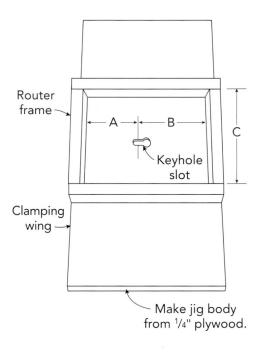

A Router Jig for Keyhole Slots

Router frame

A

B

C

Keyhole slot

Clamping wing

Make jig body from ¼" plywood.

A = radius of router subbase
B = radius of router subbase plus ¼"
C = diameter of router subbase

Using keyhole slots, even a moderately heavy cabinet can be hung on hefty screws driven into wall studs. This jig simplifies locating and routing the slots. Place the jig's precut slot over the desired location and clamp the jig to the cabinet. The frame guides the router's subbase.

2. Finish the case and back separately. I apply about four coats of wiping varnish (see "A Favorite Finish" on p. 19).
3. Tack the back into its rabbets and into the rear edges of the shelves.
4. If the cabinet will hang on a wall, rout keyhole slots into the rear edges of the case sides (see "A Router Jig for Keyhole Slots").
5. Fill the cabinet with tapes. Then kick back and enjoy the music.

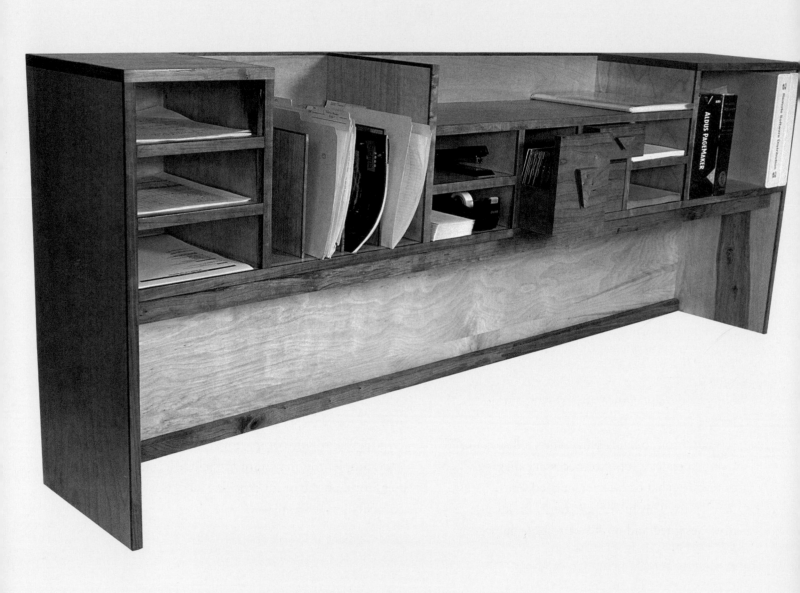

DESKTOP ORGANIZER

TO FIND THE HIGHEST concentration of clutter in your home or office, you may need go no farther than your desk. No matter how organized you are, it's likely that your desktop is piled with papers, computer disks, books, file folders, pens and pencils, envelopes, and general flotsam.

In addition to being an eyesore, a disorganized desktop creates a lot of unnecessary digging when looking for that one item you need. Fortunately, there's a fix. This birch and cherry desktop organizer, designed and built by professional wood-worker Ken Burton, serves as sort of a high-rise parking structure for desktop detritus. It provides specific storage for paper, files, pencils, binders, and more, without stealing space from the work surface. If this particular unit is too large for your desktop, you can easily alter the dimensions of the compartments to fit your particular desk. You can also tailor the function of any compartment to suit your needs. For example, you may want to include a compartment for a phone or fax machine (see "Organizing Compartments" on p. 6).

DESKTOP ORGANIZER

The case is made of ¾"-thick hardwood plywood edged with solid wood. Except for the ¼"-thick file dividers, which sit in dadoes, the case is joined with biscuits and a few pocket screws. A ¾"-thick back sits between the outermost tall dividers at the rear of the top center section. The rest of the unit gets ¼"-thick backing.

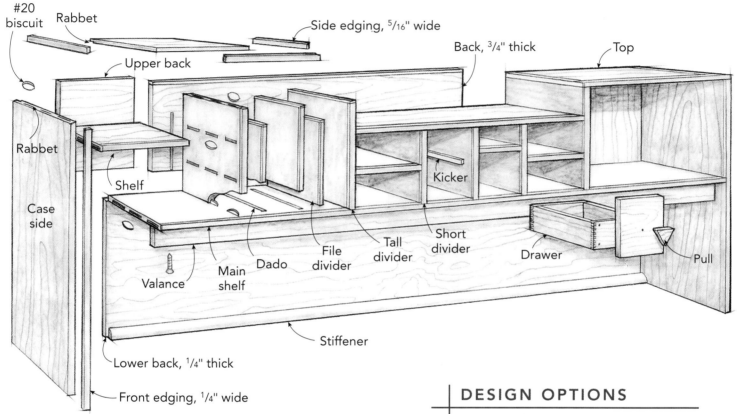

#20 biscuit

Rabbet

Side edging, 5/16" wide

Back, ³/4" thick

Top

Upper back

Rabbet

Case side

Shelf

Valance

Main shelf

Dado

File divider

Tall divider

Short divider

Kicker

Drawer

Pull

Stiffener

Lower back, 1/4" thick

Front edging, 1/4" wide

DESIGN OPTIONS

◆ Assess your particular needs and tailor compartments to suit.

◆ Construct the case with dado joints and apply edging after case assembly.

◆ Join the drawers with dovetails, rabbet-and-dado joints, or other corner joinery.

Top, Side, and Front Views

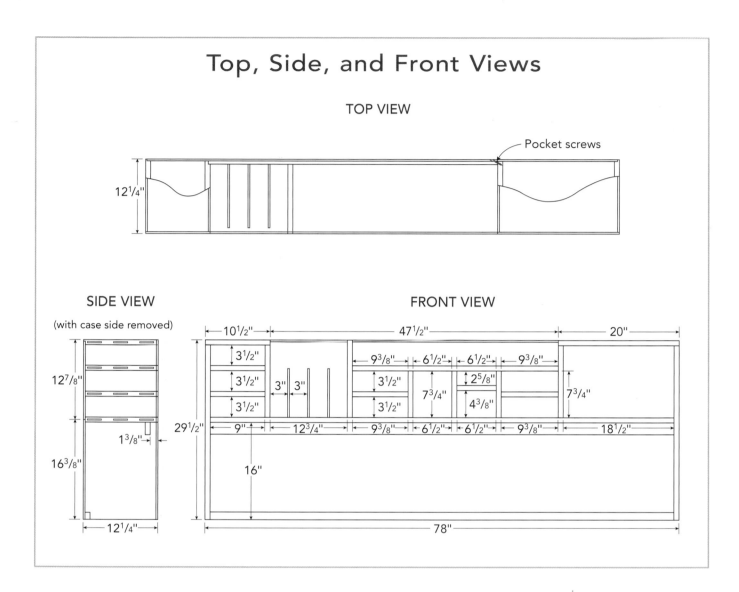

TOP VIEW

Pocket screws

12¼"

SIDE VIEW
(with case side removed)

12⅞"

1⅜"

16⅜"

12¼"

FRONT VIEW

10½" 47½" 20"

3½"
3½" 9⅜" 6½" 6½" 9⅜"
3½" 3" 3" 3½" 2⅝" 7¾"
7¾" 3½" 4⅜"
29½" 9" 12¾" 9⅜" 6½" 6½" 9⅜" 18½"

16"

78"

THE BASIC CONSTRUCTION is simple. The case is made of hardwood plywood edged with solid wood and joined with glue and biscuits. The back pieces are screwed or nailed into place. The drawers use finger-joint construction with applied fronts for a finished look.

Constructing the Case

Make the case pieces and cut the joints

Although it would be easiest to cut all the parts to finished size first, inconsistencies in plywood thickness can result in poor fits. It's best to first dry-fit the dividers and then measure between them for accurate

shelf length, dry-assembling the case as you go along.

1. Lay out the plywood case pieces.
2. Cut the pieces to size. Saw the two tops to finished length. Crosscut all of the shelves, except the main shelf, a bit oversize in length for now. Cut the back pieces a bit oversize in length also. You'll trim them all to fit later.
3. Saw or rout a ¼-in. by ½-in. rabbet in the rear edge of each top and case side to accept the ¼-in.-thick plywood backs.
4. Mill stock for the front edging. Rip the ¼-in.-wide strips from stock thicker than ¾ in. You'll trim it flush with the plywood after gluing it on. Also, rip four pieces of 5⁄16-in.-wide edging for the sides of the tops. You may need the extra bit of width

CUT LIST FOR DESKTOP ORGANIZER

Case

2	Sides	¾" x 12" x 28¾"	hardwood plywood
1	Main shelf	¾" x 11¾" x 76½"	hardwood plywood
1	Top shelf	¾" x 11¼" x 34"	hardwood plywood
2	Tall dividers	¾" x 11¾" x 12"	hardwood plywood
1	Tall divider	¾" x 11¼" x 12½"	hardwood plywood
3	Short dividers	¾" x 11¼" x 7¾"	hardwood plywood
1	Top	¾" x 12" x 10"	hardwood plywood
1	Top	¾" x 12" x 19½"	hardwood plywood
2	Shelves	¾" x 11¾" x 9"	hardwood plywood
2	Shelves	¾" x 11¼" x 9⅜"	hardwood plywood
1	Drawer divider	¾" x 11¼" x 6½"	hardwood plywood
3	File dividers	¼" x 10⅝" x 8⅜"	hardwood plywood
1	Back	¾" x 12½" x 47½"	hardwood plywood
1	Back	¼" x 12⅞" x 10¼"	hardwood plywood
1	Back	¼" x 12⅞" x 19¾"	hardwood plywood
1	Back	¼" x 16⅜" x 77½"	hardwood plywood
1	Valance	¾" x 2" x 76½"	solid wood
1	Stiffener	¾" x 1¼" x 76½"	solid wood

Drawers

2	Front/back	⅜" x 7¾" x 6½"	solid wood
2	Sides	⅜" x 7¾" x 11"	solid wood
2	Front/back	⅜" x 2⅝" x 6½"	solid wood
2	Sides	⅜" x 2⅝" x 11"	solid wood
2	Front/back	⅜" x 4⅜" x 6½"	solid wood
2	Sides	⅜" x 4⅜" x 11"	solid wood
3	Bottoms	¼" x 10⁹⁄₁₆" x 6¹⁄₁₆"	hardwood plywood
1	Drawer front	¾" x 7⅝" x 6⅜"	solid wood
1	Drawer front	¾" x 2½" x 6⅜"	solid wood
1	Drawer front	¾" x 4¼" x 6⅜"	solid wood

in the tops when fitting them flush to the sides later.

5. Glue the ⁵⁄₁₆-in.-wide edging to the side edges of both tops. After the glue cures, trim the edging flush to the plywood. To rough-trim edging, run the stock along a shim board clamped to the table saw fence (see **photo A**). Afterward, sand or scrape the edging flush the rest of the way.

6. Trim the ends of the edging flush to the front and rear edges of each top. To do this, move the rip fence shim board in front of the blade and down against the saw table (see photo F on p. 104).

7. Glue the ¼-in.-wide edging to the front edges of all the case pieces; then trim it flush to the plywood as before.

8. Lay out the spacing for the dividers using the dimensions provided. Then cut the biscuit slots for attaching them to the main shelf (see **photo B**).

9. Lay out the three 11¹⁄₁₆-in.-long dadoes in the main shelf and the mating 8³⁄₁₆-in.-long dadoes in the back to accept the ¼-in.-thick plywood file dividers. Align the end of the back with the inside edge of the left-hand divider; then clamp the back and the main shelf together for simultaneous routing (see **photo C** on p. 48). Afterward, chisel the ends of the dadoes square.

10. Dry-fit the left-hand tall divider to the main shelf and measure for the length of the two left-hand shelves. Trim the shelves to length and cut the biscuit slots for joining them to the case side and divider.

11. Dry-clamp the left-hand shelf assembly; then trim the side edges of the top piece for a flush fit with its divider and case side. Cut the biscuit joints for attaching the top.

12. Fit the right-hand top in the same manner, making sure that the divider and case side are square to the main shelf when marking the top for trimming.

13. Dry-fit the central tall divider and the short dividers; then measure for the top shelf. Cut the shelf to length and then cut

PHOTO A: To rough-trim the solid-wood edging flush to the plywood, screw a shim board to the table-saw fence with the board's face set just a hair past the outside edge of the sawteeth. Afterward, finish up with a block plane.

PHOTO B: Use a biscuit joiner to cut the biscuit slots for joining the main shelf to the case sides. All of the other case dividers and shelves are joined in the same fashion.

PHOTO C: Rout the ³⁄₁₆-in.-deep file divider dadoes in the main shelf and case back at the same time. To match the thickness of undersize ¼-in.-thick hardwood plywood, take two passes with a ³⁄₁₆-in.-diameter bit, resetting the guide fence between passes.

the biscuit slots for joining it to its tall and short dividers.

14. After measuring for the remaining shelves, trim them to length and cut the biscuit slots for attaching them to the dividers.

15. Make the ¼-in.-thick file dividers. Glue ⅛-in.-thick solid-wood edging to the front and top edges. Trim the edging ³⁄₁₆ in. from the bottom and the top rear edge to overlap the ends of the dadoes.

Assemble the case

The case assembly can be tricky because there are so many parts to put together. The best approach is to break the work into sections. Still, you may want a partner's help.

1. Glue up the center drawer/shelf section, attaching it to the main shelf. Place the dividers onto the main shelf, splaying them apart to insert the shelves and drawer dividers. Then attach the top shelf. Use plenty of clamps and cauls to pull all the parts together. Make sure everything is square under clamp pressure.

2. Attach the right-hand case side and top. Because this case is so long, it can be diffi-

cult to clamp the side to the main shelf. Burton attached it with a few pocket screws running up from under the main shelf.

3. Attach the left-hand case side and tall divider with the shelves in between. Then attach the top. Use plenty of clamps and cauls (see **photo D**).

4. Trim the ¾-in.-thick back to fit snugly between the two outermost tall dividers. When marking the trim line, ensure that the file divider dadoes in the back and the main shelf line up.

5. Attach the valance to the underside of the main shelf, setting it back from the case front 1⅜ in., as shown. Burton screwed it on from underneath through counterbored holes about 6 in. on center.

6. Fit the ¼-in.-thick backs, but don't attach them yet. Each small, upper back extends from the rabbet on the case side fully across the rear edge of the opposing tall divider. The bottom edge of each back extends halfway down the back edge of the main shelf.

7. Glue the stiffener to the lower back panel, as shown.

8. Sand the case and backs through 220 grit.

PHOTO D: Burton uses plenty of cauls and clamps to attach the left-hand section to the main shelf. Spring clamps hold cauls in place temporarily for clamping with bar clamps.

Constructing the Drawers

Make the boxes

The drawer boxes use finger joints and are made to fit the openings exactly; they are then planed or sanded to allow about ⅟₆₄-in. clearance at the top and sides. The exception is the CD drawer, which is short to allow easy access to the CDs. You can make whatever size drawers you like by following these instructions.

1. Measure the height of the drawer openings to determine the width of the drawer sides. Measure the width of the opening to determine the length of the drawer front and back pieces. To determine the length of the side pieces, measure the depth of the opening and subtract 1 in.

2. Mill the stock for the drawer boxes to ⅜ in. thick. Burton used cherry, but poplar or another secondary hardwood would be fine. Rip and crosscut the pieces to size.

3. Cut the corner joints. Burton used finger joints, but you could use rabbet-and-dado joints (see file cabinet on p. 68) or dovetails (see bed pedestal on p. 108). If making finger joints, cut the slots for a snug but easy fit. If the fingers are too tight, the glue may swell them, hindering assembly.

4. Cut the bottom grooves. If you're using finger joints, run the grooves through fingers on the sides. Then make the bottoms, allowing a total of ⅟₁₆ in. clearance between the grooves side to side and front to back.

5. Dry-assemble the drawer boxes to check the fits of the bottom and the joints. Then disassemble them, coat the corner joints thoroughly with glue, and put a couple dabs

Drawers

The solid-wood drawer boxes are joined at the corners with ¼"-wide finger joints. The ¼"-thick bottom panel rides in grooves in the box walls. The solid-wood drawer front is attached with screws.

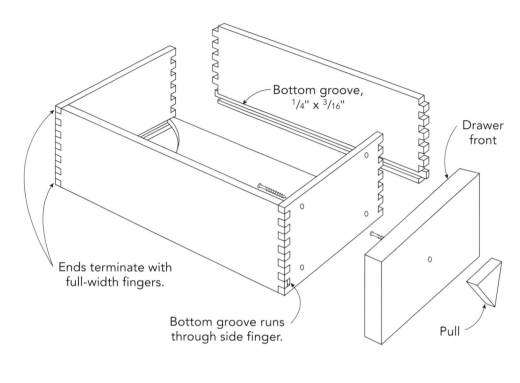

Bottom groove, ¹/₄" x ³/₁₆"

Drawer front

Ends terminate with full-width fingers.

Bottom groove runs through side finger.

Pull

of glue into the bottom grooves to prevent rattling. Clamp up the boxes, making sure they're square under clamp pressure.

6. Plane or belt sand the sides of the boxes as necessary to produce an easy, sliding fit in the drawer openings.

Make the fronts and assemble

1. Make the drawer fronts, sizing them about ¹⁄₁₆ in. less than the height and width of the drawer opening.

2. Screw the pulls to the drawer fronts. Burton made his own pulls (see "Pulls" at right), but you could use some kind of commercial pulls instead (see "Sources" on p. 172).

3. Drill four ⁹⁄₆₄-in.-diameter holes in each drawer box front for #6 screws. These "clearance holes" will allow the screws to pass freely through them, pulling the drawer front tight.

4. Apply double-sided tape to the front of the inserted drawer box; then place ¹⁄₃₂-in. shims at the bottom of the drawer opening. Center the drawer front in its opening on the shims, then press it against the tape while holding the box from behind the case.

5. Remove the drawer and attach the front to the drawer box with two #6 by 1-in. screws.

6. Reinsert the drawer and check for a consistent gap all around it. If necessary, plane the edges for an even gap or remount the fronts through the unused holes. When you're happy with the fit, install the rest of the screws.

7. Insert the drawers into their openings with the drawer fronts flush to the case front. Glue a small piece of wood to the case shelf behind each drawer to serve as a stop.

Finishing Up

1. Touch-up sand the parts if necessary. Mask the file divider dadoes and the bottom and rear edges of the file dividers to resist finish.

2. Apply finish to all of the show surfaces. Burton applied three coats of brushing lacquer, scuff sanding with steel wood before the last coat.

3. Attach two ¼-in.-thick kicker strips to the inside of the CD drawer compartment to prevent the extended drawer from tipping and to serve as drawer stops at the same time. With the drawer front set flush to the case front, lay the kickers on the drawer sides, butting them against the drawer front. Then glue and tack them in place.

4. Insert the ¾-in.-thick back between the outermost tall dividers, placing the file dividers into their glue-coated dadoes at the same time. Screw the back to the outermost case dividers with a few pocket screws, as shown in the drawing on p. 45. Then nail the back to the remaining case dividers. If the file dividers fit snugly, you won't need to clamp them in their dadoes.

5. Nail the two small ¼-in.-thick backs into place. The outer edge of each back fits into the rabbet on the case side. The inner edge lays fully across the rear edge of the tall divider.

6. Nail the large, lower back into its rabbets and the back edge of the main shelf.

TIP

When drilling holes in a drawer box to attach a drawer front, drill from the inside of the drawer whenever possible. Otherwise, the holes may be improperly angled for power-driving the screws later.

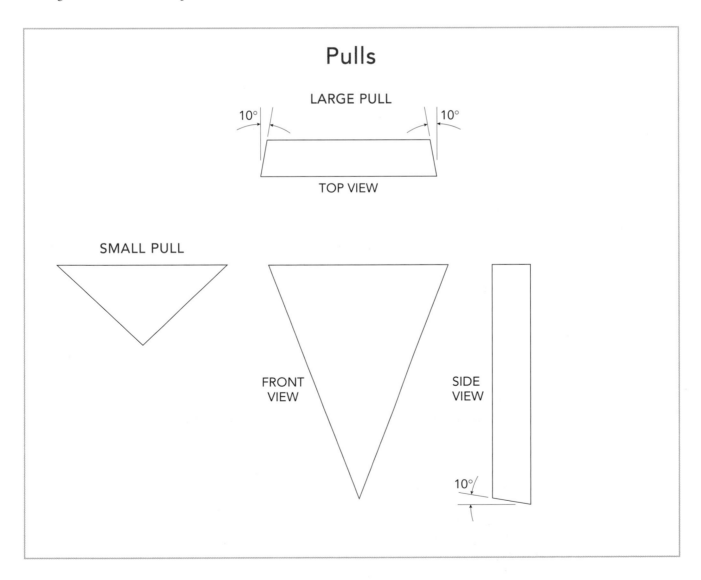

Pulls

LARGE PULL

10°   10°

TOP VIEW

SMALL PULL

FRONT VIEW   SIDE VIEW

10°

MAKING FINGER JOINTS ON THE TABLE SAW

Finger joints—also called box joints—create an incredibly strong drawer box. And they're easy to cut using a shopmade jig. At its simplest, a finger joint jig consists of a ¾-in.-thick plywood fence attached to the table saw's miter gauge. The fence has a projecting pin to register the workpiece for each successive cut.

To make the fence, fit the table saw with a dado head that's set to the width of your desired finger slots. Next, cut a slot in the fence and make a 2-in.-long wooden pin that fits the slot exactly. Glue the pin into the slot; then clamp the fence tightly to the miter gauge with

the pin a slot's width away from the sawblade. Make a few test cuts, adjusting the fence as necessary to produce snug-fitting joints. Move the pin away from the blade to make the joint tighter or toward the blade to loosen it. Then screw the fence to the miter gauge. After adjusting the fence, sawing the finger joints is a snap:

1. Place the top edge of the drawer front against the jig pin with scrap plywood behind the workpiece to minimize tearout (see top photo at right). Cut the first finger slot; then move the slot onto the pin to cut the next slot.

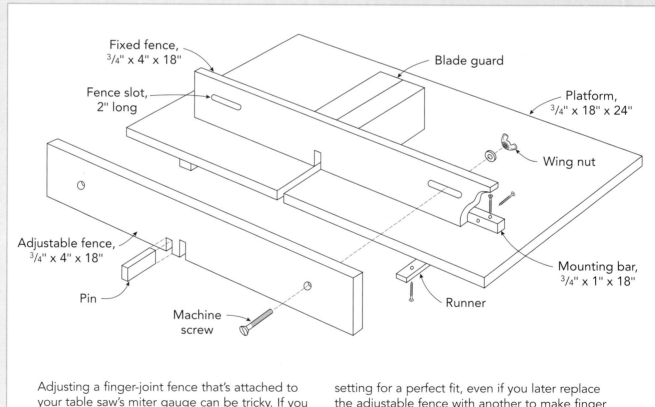

Adjusting a finger-joint fence that's attached to your table saw's miter gauge can be tricky. If you make finger joints often, it's worth making a jig like this. It allows you to easily fine-tune the pin setting for a perfect fit, even if you later replace the adjustable fence with another to make finger joints of a different width.

Repeat for remaining slots. When cutting joints on the opposite end and on the drawer back, always begin with the top edge resting against the pin.

2. Place the uppermost slot of the drawer front over the pin and nestle the top of the drawer side against the front, as shown in the bottom photo above. Make the first cut, which is a notch rather than a slot. Then push the notch against the pin to saw the following slot. At this point, complete the joint in the same manner as described in step 1.

PRINTER STAND

There are certain pieces of equipment, such as computer peripherals and stereo components, that require a sort of open storage. That is, they need a dedicated space to sit while remaining constantly accessible. A printer for a computer is a good example. It needs to sit out in the open near the computer for feeding and retrieving paper. Because of that, it usually ends up on the desktop, where it takes up precious real estate.

The obvious solution is to place the printer on its own dedicated stand of some sort. You could use a table, but that wastes space in a crowded office. Instead, it makes sense to employ the area underneath for storing the printer's "baggage"—usually several reams of various types of paper. In fact, a printer stand is also great place to stash envelopes and notepads along with other office accoutrements, such as computer disks and CDs.

Professional woodworker Ken Burton designed and built this solid cherry printer stand, which includes adjustable shelves to house paper, envelopes, and computer disks. The stand features doors with tapered rails and stiles, a curved crest rail, ebony plugs, and shaped pulls. A sawn opening in the crest rail serves as a port for cable access. Burton's printer is 17 in. wide by 14 in. deep. If you have or plan to buy a larger model, adjust the width and depth of the stand to suit your machine.

PRINTER STAND

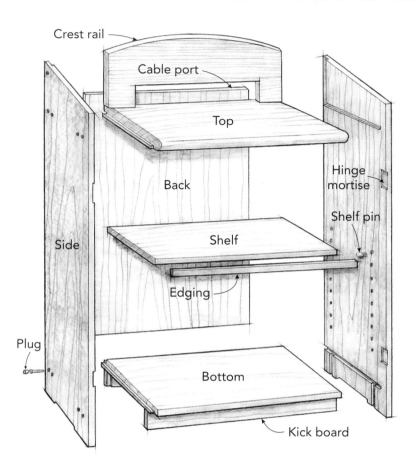

Crest rail

Cable port

Top

Hinge mortise

Back

Shelf pin

Side

Shelf

Edging

Plug

Bottom

Kick board

The case joinery consists primarily of tongues on the horizontal pieces that fit into dadoes and grooves in the case sides. The crest rail and back simply fit into rabbets cut into the rear edges of the case sides. The large cable port allows room for projecting cable plugs. The raised kick boards and lower cutouts on the sides allow the case to sit on four "feet" for good stability.

The door frames are joined with loose tenons. The solid-wood panels are rabbeted to create tongues that fit into grooves cut in the door frames.

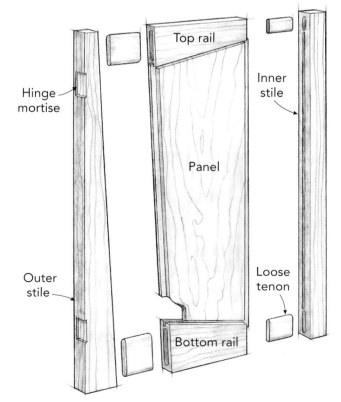

Top rail

Inner stile

Hinge mortise

Panel

Outer stile

Loose tenon

Bottom rail

DESIGN OPTIONS

- Outfit the inside of the cabinet with custom dividers and pigeonholes.

- Design the door stiles and rails to match existing cabinetry.

- Incorporate a drawer into the cabinet.

- Use hardwood plywood for the case and door panels.

Top, Side, and Front Views of Printer Stand

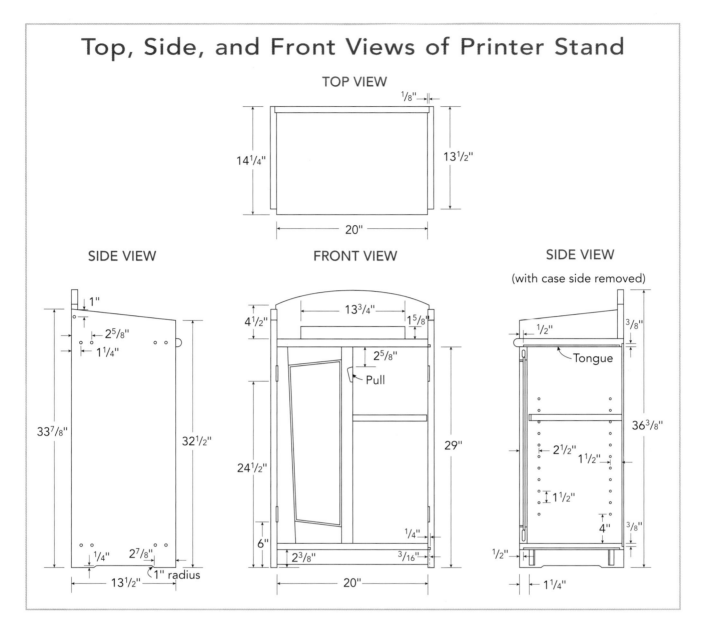

TOP VIEW

SIDE VIEW

FRONT VIEW

SIDE VIEW
(with case side removed)

Constructing the Case

This cabinet is made from solid wood, so the first step is to make the panels for the parts. After that, you'll cut the joints, drill the shelf holes, and assemble the case.

Prepare the parts

1. Make the solid-wood panels for the sides, top, and bottom. Pick attractive boards for the sides. If you have to edge-join narrower boards to make the panels, lay them out for consistent grain and color match (see "Composing Grain for Panels" on p. 99).

2. Plane and rip the stock for the kick boards and crest rail. Leave the pieces slightly oversize in length for now. You'll crosscut them for a perfect fit after assembling the case.

3. After flattening and smoothing any joined-up panels, lay out the angle at the top of each side and the profile at the bottom.

4. Cut the angle at the top of each side. Remember that there's a left and a right, and that you'll want to keep the good sides facing

AS WHEN MAKING ANY cabinet with inset doors, it's necessary to make the case first so that the doors can be fit precisely into their openings.

Front and Side Views of Doors

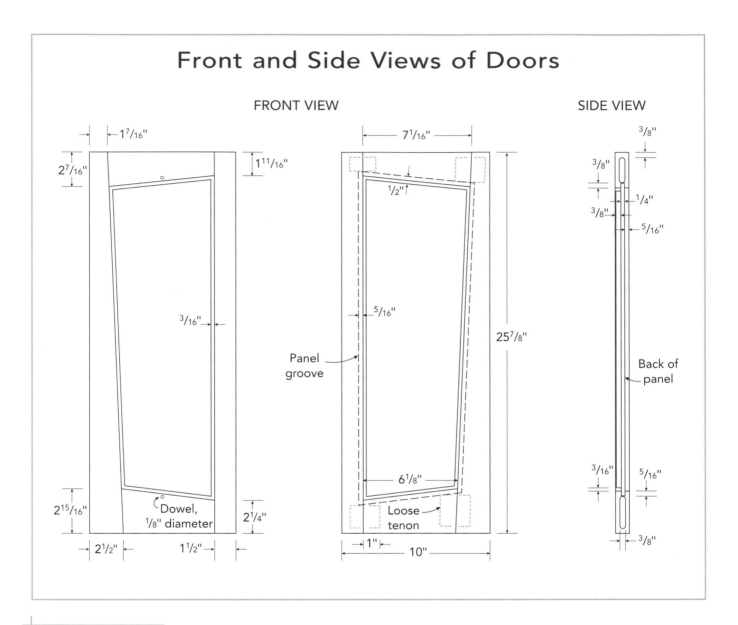

FRONT VIEW

1⁷/₁₆"

2⁷/₁₆"

1¹¹/₁₆"

3/₁₆"

2¹⁵/₁₆"

Dowel,
⅛" diameter

2¼"

2½"   1½"

7¹/₁₆"

½"

5/₁₆"

Panel
groove

25⁷/₈"

6⅛"

Loose
tenon

1"   10"

SIDE VIEW

3/₈"

3/₈"

¼"

3/₈"

5/₁₆"

Back of
panel

3/₁₆"   5/₁₆"

3/₈"

TIP

When laying out parts, select the nicest-looking boards for the most prominent surfaces. Consider how a piece of furniture will be viewed in place. For the typical base cabinet, the front and top are the most prominent, followed by the sides.

outward. Burton uses a commercial after-market miter gauge with a long extension fence to make the cut. Alternatively, you could tack a temporary fence onto a crosscut sled or cut the angle with a jigsaw or portable circular saw guided by a wood fence clamped to the workpiece.

5. Cut the profile at the bottom of each side that creates the "feet." First shape the ends using a 1-in.-diameter drill bit. Then cut the remaining straight section with a jigsaw. You could also make a hardboard template of the shape and use it to guide a router outfitted with a template guide. Chamfer the bottom

edges of the feet slightly to prevent tearout when dragging the cabinet.

6. Lay out the curve on the crest rail. To get a fair curve, spring a thin strip of straight-grained wood to the proper curvature (see "Springing a Curve" on p. 101).

7. Cut the curve with a jigsaw or bandsaw or use a router guided by a custom template. Then sand the curve smooth.

8. Cut the plywood shelves to size; then make the solid-wood edging strips and apply them to the front edge of each shelf (see photo A on p. 47).

Make the joints

1. Lay out the ¼-in.-wide dadoes in the sides to accept the tongues you'll cut on the ends of the top and bottom. The bottom groove is 2⅜ in. up from the bottom, and the top groove is 29 in. up from the bottom.

2. Rout the dadoes 5/16 in. deep, guiding the router with a straightedge (see photo C on p. 48).

3. Lay out the ⅝-in.-wide grooves in the sides to accept the kick boards. The grooves run all the way to the bottom of each side, although the kick board doesn't. Then rout the 3/16-in.-deep grooves, again guiding the router with a straightedge.

4. Cut the rabbets on the ends of the top and bottom pieces to create the ¼-in.-thick by ¼-in.-long tongues. Burton does this on the router table, feeding the workpiece on end against the fence (see **photo A** on p. 60). Instead, you could make the cuts on the table saw. Aim for a snug fit in the dadoes.

5. Use a handsaw to trim away the front section of each tongue to match the length of the stopped dado. Clean up the sawn surface with a chisel if necessary.

6. Rout the ¼-in.-wide by ⅜-in.-deep rabbets in the rear edges of the sides and top and bottom to accept the ¼-in.-thick back panel. Dry-assemble the case pieces to determine where to stop the rabbets on the case sides.

7. Lay out and rout the ¾-in.-wide by ⅛-in.-deep rabbets in the rear edges of the sides to accept the ends of the crest rail.

CUT LIST FOR PRINTER STAND

Case			
2	Sides	¾" x 13½" x 33⅞"	solid wood
1	Top	1" x 14¼" x 20½"	solid wood
1	Bottom	¾" x 13½" x 20½"	solid wood
2	Kick boards	¾" x 2" x 20⅜"	solid wood
1	Crest rail	¾" x 6⅜" x 20¼"	solid wood
1	Back	¼" x 20¾" x 26⅝"	hardwood plywood
4	Shelves	¾" x 11¾" x 19⅞"	hardwood plywood
4	Shelf edgings	¼" x ¾" x 19⅞"	solid wood
Doors			
2	Outer stiles	1" x 2½" x 25⅞"	solid wood
2	Inner stiles	1" x 1½" x 25⅞"	solid wood
2	Top rails	1" x 2 7/16" x 7 3/16"	solid wood
2	Bottom rails	1" x 2 15/16" x 6¼"	solid wood
2	Panels	⅝" x 7¾" x 22 11/16"	solid wood
2	Pulls	¾" x ¾" x 2"	solid wood
Other materials			
4	Butt hinges	2" x ⅞"	*from* Rockler; item #32926
16	Shelf support pins	¼"	*from* Rockler; item #30437
2	Brass ball catches	1¾" x 5/16"	*from* Rockler; item #28613

Cut the hinge mortises in the case

An attractive, well-hung door depends on good-quality hinges that fit well in properly cut mortises. With a bit of careful work, you can install hinges that fit sweetly in their mortises and create perfect planar alignment of a door with its frame. Before you mortise your project, it's wise to cut two mating mortises in scrap, then temporarily join them with a hinge to check the gap between the two pieces.

1. Position the hinge so that its pin projects just beyond the case front.

2. Hold the hinge down firmly and scribe around the perimeter of the leaf with a sharp knife (see **photo B** on p. 60). Make your first pass a light one to prevent shoving the hinge. Deepen the outline on the second pass.

3. Adjust a your router so a straight bit projects 1/32 in. below the center of the hinge pin (see "Bit Adjustment for Routing a Hinge Mortise" on p. 62). This will create a 1/16-in. gap between the door and its frame. For less of a gap, increase the bit projection accordingly.

4. Rout the majority of the waste from the mortise, staying 1/16 in. or so inside the scribed lines (see **photo C**).

PHOTO A: Cut the rabbet on each end of the top and bottom piece to create the ¼-in. by ¼-in. tongue. Cutting the rabbets on the router table as shown here ensures a tongue of consistent thickness.

PHOTO B: Hold the hinge down firmly and scribe around the perimeter of the leaf with a sharp knife. Make your first pass a light one to prevent shoving the hinge. Deepen the outline on the second pass.

5. Using a very sharp chisel, pare back to your scribed outline, cutting downward to the depth of the mortise bottom (see **photo D**). Remove the waste by paring it away from the bottom of the mortise, moving toward the edges (see **photo E**).

6. After you slice away all bits of remaining wood inside the scribed outline, the hinge should fit perfectly (see **photo F**).

Assemble the case

1. Dry-clamp the top and bottom between the sides to make sure the joints draw up tightly and the pieces all properly align.

2. With the case still clamped, measure for the back and cut it to fit snugly within its rabbets.

3. Drill and counterbore the holes in the case sides for securing the top and bottom into their dadoes with #10 by 2½-in. flat-head screws.

4. Glue the case sides to the top and bottom. Place the unglued back into its rabbets to help hold the case square while drying. Lay the case on its back on a flat surface and compare the diagonal measurements across the front. If necessary, pull the case into square by applying clamp pressure diagonally across the front.

5. Measure between the kick board grooves and cut the kick boards to length. Then glue and clamp the pieces to the case bottom and sides.

6. Trim the crest rail to fit within its rabbets, then saw the cable port.

7. Attach the crest rail, gluing it to the top and screwing it to the sides.

TIP

Good-quality extruded brass hinges are more expensive than the stamped hinges typically found in hardware stores, but they look and work much better. They're beefier, stronger, and the pins won't slop around in the knuckle like in the stamped steel jobs.

PHOTO C: When routing the waste from the mortise, stay ¹⁄₁₆ in. or so inside the scribed lines.

PHOTO D: With a chisel, pare back to the scribed outline and then cut down to the full depth of the mortise.

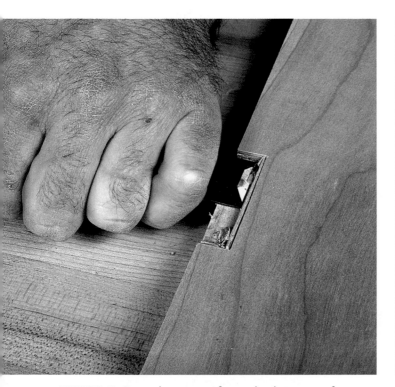

PHOTO E: Pare the waste from the bottom of the mortise.

PHOTO F: The hinge should fit perfectly.

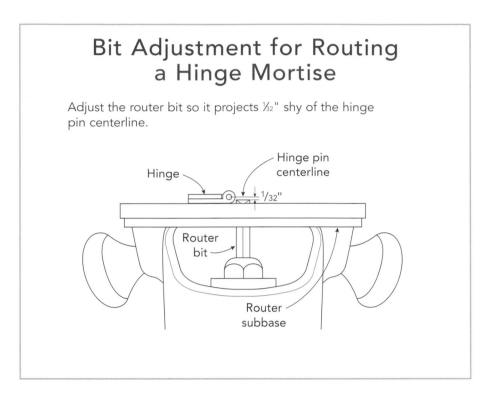

Bit Adjustment for Routing a Hinge Mortise

Adjust the router bit so it projects ¹⁄₃₂" shy of the hinge pin centerline.

Hinge

Hinge pin centerline

¹⁄₃₂"

Router bit

Router subbase

PHOTO G: After assembling the case, Burton glues the ebony plugs into the counterbored screw holes.

PHOTO H: Burton uses a shopmade drilling template to save layout time and ensure that the shelf support holes are spaced accurately.

8. Make the plugs for filling the counterbored screw holes. Although Burton used plugs made of ebony, you could use any contrasting or matching wood. Glue the plugs into their holes (see **photo G**). After the glue dries, trim the plugs flush.

9. Drill the holes for the shelf supports. A shopmade template makes quick work of this and ensures accurate spacing (see **photo H**).

10. Make the shelves. Burton used ¾-in.-thick birch plywood edged with solid wood.

Constructing the Doors

Now that the case is built, you can make the doors for an exact fit. If you like, you could forego making the tapered frame doors in favor of doors that match your existing office cabinetry. But if you want to give it

a try, you'll find the tapered stiles and rails aren't all that difficult to make. The technique provides a method to account for small errors in the rail angles so that the doors still come together correctly. You'll cut the rail angles, do the joinery, and then glue the rails onto the straight stiles before attaching the angled stiles. You'll cancel out any small errors in that assembly by passing it lightly by the sawblade so that the rail faces are cut parallel to the door sides. The final stile is not tapered, so the assembly ends up being very similar to any other door.

Make the parts

1. Begin by making a full-size drawing of the door so you'll be able to take direct measurements from it for the various angles and tapers.

TIP

When installing wood plugs, be sure to orient the grain of the plugs parallel to the grain of the workpiece so that the wood of both will move in the same direction. This also helps disguise plugs that aren't of a contrasting wood.

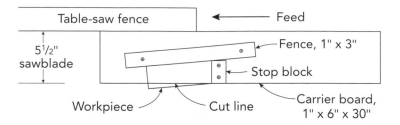

Tapering Jig

Table-saw fence

← Feed

Fence, 1" x 3"

5½"
sawblade

Stop block

Workpiece — Cut line

Carrier board,
1" x 6" x 30"

This three-piece jig consists of a fence, a stop block, and a carrier board with straight, parallel sides. To use it, set your fence to the width of the carrier board and align your cut line to the edge of the carrier board, as shown. Screw the fence and stop block against the workpiece and you're ready to cut.

2. Mill the square blanks for the rails and stiles. Leave the rails about ¼-in. oversize in length for now. Mill the panels to ⅝ in. thick, but leave them oversize in width and length.

3. Lay out the rails and stiles for a pleasing grain pattern and mark them for orientation (see "The Triangle Marking System" on p. 18).

4. Trimming away as little as possible, square the end of each rail that abuts the center stile.

5. Referring to your full-size plans, lay out the tapers on the rails and outer stiles.

6. Saw the tapers. Burton uses a simple, shopmade tapering jig for the job (see "Tapering Jig"). You'll need to reset the jig for each pair of top and bottom rails, because their tapers differ.

7. Again using your full-size pattern, lay out the tapered ends on the rails; then crosscut at that angle, about ⅛ in. outside of your cut line. You'll do the final trimming after assembling the rails to the inner stiles.

Cut the joints and assemble the doors

1. Lay out the ⅜-in.-wide mortises on the stiles and rails. The length of each rail mortise extends to within ⅜ in. from the edge of the rail.

2. Rout the mortises to a depth of 1 in. Use a router edge guide to center the mortises across the thickness of the stock. A jig can be very helpful when routing mortises in the ends of rails (see "Router Mortising Jig" on p. 74).

3. Mill lengths of stock from which to crosscut the individual tenons. Rip the stock to a width about ⅛ in. less than the length of its mortise. Then plane the tenon stock so it slides into the mortise with just a bit of finger pressure. After routing or planing a bull-nose profile on both edges of the stock, crosscut the individual tenons to length.

4. Rout the ⁵⁄₁₆-in.-deep by ¼-in.-wide grooves in all of the rails and stiles to accept the door panels (see **photo I**). Space the groove ⁵⁄₁₆ in. away from the rear face of each rail or stile and stop it just short of each frame mortise.

5. Dry-assemble each rail to its outermost stile to make sure that the corners of the frame are square and that the tenons aren't too long. If necessary, trim the rail ends or tenons.

6. Glue and clamp each top and bottom rail to its outermost stile. Make sure the outer edge of each rail aligns with the end of its stile and that the joints are pulled fully home along their length. Let the glue dry thoroughly after wiping off any excess.

7. Set your table-saw rip fence for an 8½-in. cut; then trim the inner ends of the rails to perfect length by feeding the frame assembly through the table saw (see **photo J**). This will reduce the depth of the mortise a bit, but you'll cut the length of your loose tenon to suit.

8. Saw the door panels to shape and size, taking measurements directly from the frame. When ripping them to width,

PHOTO I: Rout the ¼-in.-wide by ⁵⁄₁₆-in.-deep door panel grooves using a slotting cutter on the router table.

PHOTO J: After gluing the rails to the tapered outer stiles, feed the door frame assembly through the table saw to trim the innermost ends of the rails, creating a perfect fit against the edges of the inner stile.

PHOTO K: Replace the door in its opening, straddling a couple of ¾4-in.-thick shims. Use a sharp knife to lay out each hinge into the front edge of the stile.

remember to allow for wood movement across the grain.

9. Saw or rout the ⅜-in.-deep by ½-in.-wide rabbets in the front edges of the panels. This will create a ¼-in.-thick by ½-in.-wide tongue on the edges of the panels to fit into the grooves in the door frame.

10. Slip the panels into their grooves and dry-assemble the innermost stiles to their rails to check the fit of the joints and panel.

11. Pre-finish the panels to prevent bare wood from showing when the panels shrink. Sand the inside edges of the stiles and rails through 220 grit.

12. Place the unglued panels in their grooves; then glue and clamp the stiles to the rails. Make sure the assemblies lie flat while under clamp pressure to prevent twisting the doors. To keep each panel centered in its frame, Burton pins them with two ⅛-in.-diameter dowels through the rear of the frame into the panel.

13. Sand the front and rear faces of the doors through 220 grit. Don't worry about the edges for now.

Attach the doors and pulls

Flush-mounted doors are one of the emblems of quality cabinetry. Although more difficult to install than overlay doors, they impart much more elegance to a piece. Here's how to correctly install them flush to the case with a small gap of consistent width between the doors and the cabinet opening.

1. Begin by cutting the hinge mortises in the case. (This is often done before case

TIP

To prevent snapping the brass screws, drill pilot holes and temporarily install a steel screw in each hole to thread it before driving in the brass screws. To lubricate the screws, use wax. Don't use soap, as some woodworkers suggest, because soap attracts moisture and invites corrosion.

assembly because the case top and bottom can impede router access afterward.)

2. Trim the door to fit the dimensions of the case opening minus 1⁄16 in. in length and width. Set the door into its opening, resting on the case bottom but pressed against the case side. Note any gaps along the bottom edge; then plane the bottom of the door until the stile and bottom rail sit entirely flush against the case side and bottom.

3. Install the hinges into their case mortises with one center screw per hinge. Offset the screws very slightly to draw the hinge leaf against the rear wall of the mortise.

4. Replace the door in its opening, straddling a couple of dimes or other 3⁄64-in.-thick shims. Press the door stile against the folded hinges and run a sharp knife along the top edge of each hinge and into the front edge of the stile (see **photo K**).

5. Remove the door and align a hinge to your knife mark with the axis of the hinge pin projecting just beyond the case front. Trace around the hinge leaf with a sharp knife; then rout and chisel the mortises.

6. Install the door with one center screw per hinge, again offsetting the screws slightly to draw the hinge leaf against the rear wall of the mortise.

7. To establish the trim line at the top of the door, make a mark at each upper corner of the door 3⁄32 in. away from the case top. Remove the door, connect the marks using a ruler, and then plane to the trim line.

8. Reattach the doors and check the gaps for consistency. Use a handplane to make any corrections.

9. Sand the edges of the doors through 220 grit and ease all of the corners slightly.

10. Make the pulls. Draw each front profile on 3⁄4-in.-thick stock; then bandsaw and sand to the lines. Next, draw the side profile on the outermost edge of each pull and bandsaw to the line, laying the flat edge of the pull on the bandsaw table. Finish up by sanding the rear of the pulls.

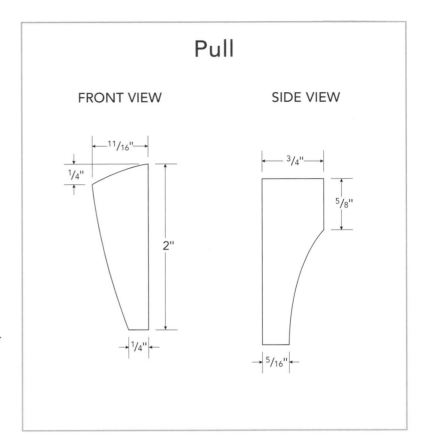

Pull

FRONT VIEW

SIDE VIEW

11. Glue and screw the pulls to the doors, positioning them 2⅝ in. down from the tops of the doors.

Finishing Up

1. Remove the doors and hinges. Do any necessary touchup sanding to all exposed surfaces.

2. If you like, stain the birch plywood shelves to match the color of your case wood.

3. Apply the finish of your choice. Burton wiped on three coats of an antique oil finish, scuffing with 0000 steel wool between coats.

4. Attach the hinges and reinstall the doors, using all the hinge screws this time.

5. Install the brass ball catches to the case top and center stile of each door.

6. Install the shelf support pins and shelves. Then load up the cabinet and click "print"!

TIP

Avoid using magnetic catches of any sort near computer disks. The magnetic field can harm digital data.

INSET: For a traditional look, the cabinet can be made with a solid-wood beveled drawer front and brass hardware.

FILE CABINET

WHEN IT COMES TO STORING life's paperwork, it's hard to beat a file cabinet. There's no better way to organize your bills, correspondence, bank statements, catalogs, drawings, clippings, etc., while keeping everything accessible.

This heavy-duty file cabinet is easy to build. I designed it to be made of ¾-in.-thick birch plywood with a solid-wood face frame. The plywood top is made separately and screwed to the case. The drawer boxes are made of ½-in.-thick plywood, joined with rabbet-and-dado joints at the corners. The drawer fronts are plywood, edged with solid wood. The drawer pull is an integral part of the drawer edging. Full extension "overtravel" drawer slides allow easy access to the rearmost files in a drawer.

You can easily modify this cabinet to suit your particular needs. You can make it taller or deeper to hold more files. The length of the drawers are determined by the length of the drawer slides you choose.

FILE CABINET

This heavy-duty file cabinet is constructed of ¾"-thick hardwood plywood with a solid-wood face frame and edging. The face frame is constructed with loose tenon joints. The drawer slide shims allow mounting of commercial full-extension slides.

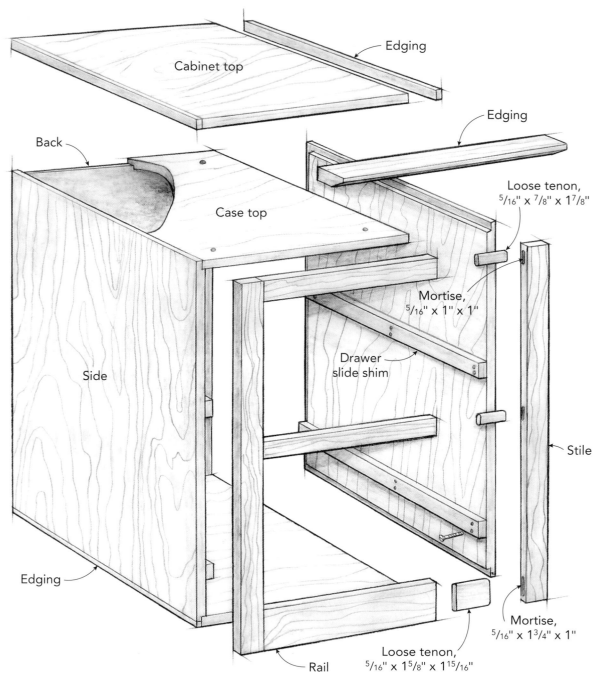

Edging

Cabinet top

Edging

Back

Loose tenon,
$^5/_{16}$" x $^7/_8$" x $1^7/_8$"

Case top

Mortise,
$^5/_{16}$" x 1" x 1"

Drawer
slide shim

Side

Stile

Edging

Mortise,
$^5/_{16}$" x $1^3/_4$" x 1"

Rail

Loose tenon,
$^5/_{16}$" x $1^5/_8$" x $1^{15}/_{16}$"

Not to scale

Side and Front Views

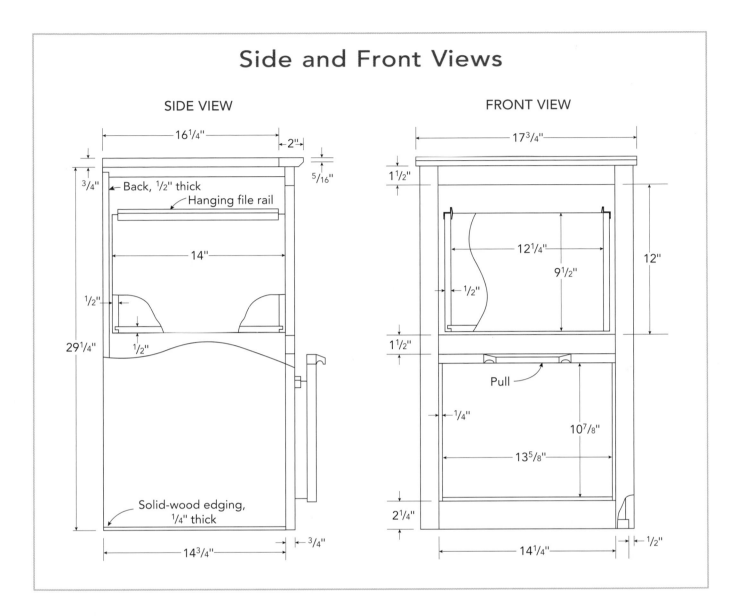

SIDE VIEW

FRONT VIEW

16¼"

2"

⁵⁄₁₆"

¾"

Back, ½" thick

Hanging file rail

14"

½"

½"

29¼"

Solid-wood edging, ¼" thick

14¾"

¾"

17¾"

1½"

12¼"

9½"

½"

12"

1½"

Pull

¼"

10⅞"

13⅝"

2¼"

14¼"

½"

DESIGN OPTIONS

+ For a traditional look, make beveled, solid-wood drawer fronts, using commercially available brass pulls and card holders.

+ For legal-size files, make the cabinet and drawers 3 in. wider than shown.

+ Make an instant desk by placing a separate top across two file cabinets.

BUILD THE CASE and face frame first. Then make the drawer boxes and install them. Last, make and attach the drawer fronts and cabinet top.

Building the Case

Make the plywood box

1. Lay out and cut the cabinet top, case sides, case top, case bottom, and back to size.
2. Mark the pieces for orientation (see "Triangle Marking System" on p. 18).
3. Mill the ¼-in. by ¾-in. solid-wood edging for the bottoms of the sides. The edging protects the plywood from tearout when moving the cabinet.

CUT LIST FOR FILE CABINET

2	Sides	¾" x 14¾" x 29"	hardwood plywood
2	Case top/bottom	¾" x 14¾" x 29"	hardwood plywood
1	Top	¾" x 14¼" x 17¼"	hardwood plywood
1	Back	½" x 16¼" x 28¼"	hardwood plywood
2	Side/bottom edgings	¾" x ¼" x 14¾"	solid wood
1	Top edging	¾" x 2" x 17¾"	solid wood
2	Top edgings	¾" x ¼" x 14¼"	solid wood
2	Stiles	¾" x 1¹⁷⁄₃₂" x 29¼"	solid wood
2	Rails	¾" x 1½" x 14¼"	solid wood
1	Rail	¾" x 2¼" x 14¼"	solid wood
4	Drawer slide shims	¾" x 2½" x 14⅛"	solid wood
2	Drawer fronts	¾" x 10⅞" x 13⅝"	hardwood plywood
4	Drawer sides	½" x 9½" x 14"	hardwood plywood
4	Drawer front/backs	½" x 9½" x 12¾"	hardwood plywood
2	Drawer bottoms	½" x 13½" x 12¾"	hardwood plywood
2	Pulls	¾" x 1½" x 14⅛"	solid wood
2	Drawer front edgings	¾" x ¼" x 13⅝"	solid wood
4	Drawer front edgings	¾" x ¼" x 11⅛"	solid wood

Other materials

2 pairs	Overtravel drawer slides	14"	*from* Woodworker's Hardware item #KV8505 14
1	Hanging file rail	2.5m	*from* Woodworker's Hardware; item #CPF32500

TIP

Hardwood plywood often varies from its nominal thickness. To ensure accurate overall dimensions, measure the positive half of a cut joint, not the negative space. For example, when cutting the ¼-in.-deep rabbets in ¾-in.-thick case sides, make sure that the tongue is ½ in. thick, regardless of the depth.

4. Glue the edging to the sides; then plane or scrape it flush to the plywood after the glue cures.

5. Cut the ¼ in. by ¾ in. rabbets in the top and bottom edges of the sides. I do this on the table saw, using a dado head (see **photo A**). Set up the cut using scrap from the same plywood sheet that yielded the sides.

6. Reset the rip fence for a ½-in.-wide cut, but leave the height of the dado head as is. Then cut the rabbets in the rear edges of all the case pieces to accept the ½-in.-thick plywood back.

7. Dry-clamp the case and make sure the back fits into its rabbets. The closer the fit, the better, as the back will help square up the case during glue-up.

8. Unclamp the case and apply glue to both halves of each joint. Clamp up the case using thick hardwood cauls to distribute pressure across the joints. Make sure the clamp screws align with the case top and bottom to prevent bowing in the case sides. Place the back unglued into its rabbets to hold the case square while the glue cures.

9. Mill the edging stock for the cabinet top. Rip the pieces from a board that you've planed to about ¹⁄₃₂ in. thicker than your plywood.

10. Glue the side edging on first, then plane or scrape it flush to the plywood after the glue cures. Next, glue on the front edging and plane it flush to the plywood.

11. Mark the 45-degree chamfer on the end of the front edging. Rip the chamfer on the table saw; then plane or sand off any saw marks.

Make and attach the face frame

1. Cut the stiles and rails to size. To ensure a flat, square face frame, joint the inside edges of the stiles square and crosscut the rails accurately. Mill extra stock for tool setup.

2. Lay out the pieces for a pleasing grain pattern and mark them for orientation.

3. Cut the face frame joints. I used loose tenon joinery, which consists of two mating mortises that accept a separately made tenon. I routed the mortises using a shop-made jig (see "Router Mortising Jig" on

PHOTO A: After applying protective solid-wood edging to the bottom of the side pieces, saw the rabbets in the top and bottom edges using a dado head and an auxiliary rip fence.

p. 74). Alternatively, you could join the face frame using biscuits, pocket screws, or dowels.

4. Rip long strips for the tenons from stock that you've planed to fit the mortises snugly. Round over the edges of the tenon stock on the router table to match approximately the radius of the mortises. Then cut the individual tenons to length.

5. Glue up the face frame on a flat surface, carefully aligning the rails with the ends of the stiles (see **photo B**). Make sure that the drawer openings are 12 in. high.

6. After the glue cures, plane or belt sand both faces of the frame. To ensure a good glue joint against the case, make certain that the rear face is very flat.

7. Make the drawer slide shims.

8. With the cabinet back sitting unglued in its rabbets and the drawer slide shims temporarily in place, attach the face frame. Make sure the drawer slide shims are equally aligned with the inside edges of the stiles before tightening the clamps.

PHOTO B: To ease assembly, connect and align one half of the face frame before the glue sets up tack. Then glue on the other stile. The ¾-in.-diameter dowels center the clamp pressure on the stiles, preventing them from buckling under clamp pressure.

ROUTER MORTISING JIG

In a typical loose tenon joint, a mortise is routed into the edge of one member (in this case the stile) and a mating mortise is routed into the end of the other member (here, the rail). A separately made tenon is then glued into the mortises to create a very strong joint.

Edge mortises are easy to rout using a standard router edge guide. However, end mortises require a jig to hold the workpiece vertical and provide router support. The mortising jig shown here allows you to rout edge mortises and end mortises with the same edge guide setting. Router-travel stops ensure mortises of matching length. The vertical fence can be installed at an angle for routing mortises in the ends of mitered pieces. Here's how the jig works to cut face frame joints.

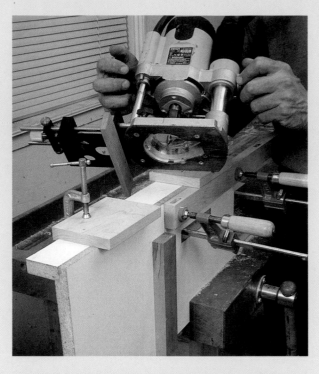

1. Mark the rail spacing on the inner edges of your face frame stiles. Then lay out one stile mortise.

2. Mount an upcut spiral bit of the proper diameter in the router.

3. Clamp the stile to the jig so the stile's inner edge is aligned with the top edge of the jig. (Important: To ensure flush joints, always place the inner face of a workpiece against the face of the jig.) Align the rail position mark (or end of the stile when appropriate) with a line drawn upward from the jig's fence (see photo above). Then clamp the router-travel stops in place.

4. Adjust the router edge guide to locate the bit over the marked-out mortise. Position the bit at one end of the mortise and clamp a stop against the appropriate side of the router base. Slide the router to the opposite end of the mortise and clamp the other stop in place.

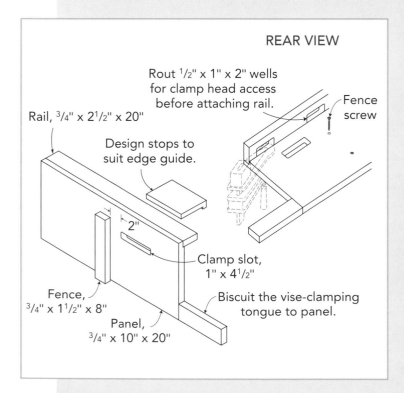

REAR VIEW

Rout 1/2" x 1" x 2" wells for clamp head access before attaching rail.

Fence screw

Rail, 3/4" x 2 1/2" x 20"

Design stops to suit edge guide.

2"

Clamp slot, 1" x 4 1/2"

Fence, 3/4" x 1 1/2" x 8"

Panel, 3/4" x 10" x 20"

Biscuit the vise-clamping tongue to panel.

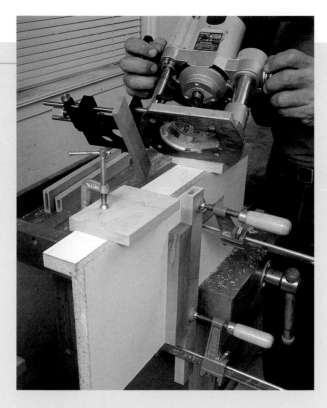

5. Rout the mortise in successive passes, pushing the router away from you with the edge guide to your right. Maintain firm downward pressure on the half of the router that rides on the jig.

6. Rout all other stile mortises of the same length in the same manner.

7. To set up to rout the mating mortises, clamp a rail in place against the jig's fence and flush to the top of the jig (see photo above). Without changing the position of the stops, rout the mortise. Repeat for all other rail mortises of the same length.

8. To rout mortises of a different length, simply adjust the position of the right-hand stop; then rout the matching stile and rail mortises in the same manner as above.

This process reads more complicated than it is. Once you've completed one set of joints using this jig, you'll find the process very efficient.

9. Using a flush-trimming bit, rout the stile overhang flush to the sides of the case.

Building the Drawers

The drawers are simple plywood boxes. The drawer fronts are made separately and then attached with screws after installing the drawer boxes into the case.

Make the boxes

1. Cut the plywood pieces for the drawer boxes. Accurate sawing here makes a big difference in the fit and installation of the drawers, so work carefully.

2. Mark the parts for orientation;, then sand their inside faces. Sanding after cutting the joints can ruin the joint fit. Use a flat sanding block, being careful not to round over the edges.

3. Cut the drawer joints as shown in "Quick 'n' Easy Drawer Joints" on p. 77.

4. After doing a dry clamp-up to make sure all the parts fit well, glue up the drawer boxes on a flat surface (see **photo C** on p. 76). I just spot glue the bottoms, applying a dab of glue in the center of each groove.

5. Sand the joints on the front of each box flush.

Make the drawer fronts

1. Working as accurately as possible, cut the plywood for the drawer fronts.

2. Make the edging pieces and the blanks for the pulls. I plane the stock for the edging about $\frac{1}{32}$ in. thicker than the plywood. Then I rip the strips slightly oversize, plane them to $\frac{1}{4}$ in., and crosscut them about $\frac{1}{16}$ in. oversize in length

3. Glue the bottom edging in place. I use bar clamps to pull both drawer fronts together with their bottom edges butting. After the glue cures, pare the ends flush with a very sharp chisel, and plane and scrape the faces flush.

4. Apply the side edging in a similar manner; then trim it flush to the plywood. Sand the face of the drawer front through 220 grit.

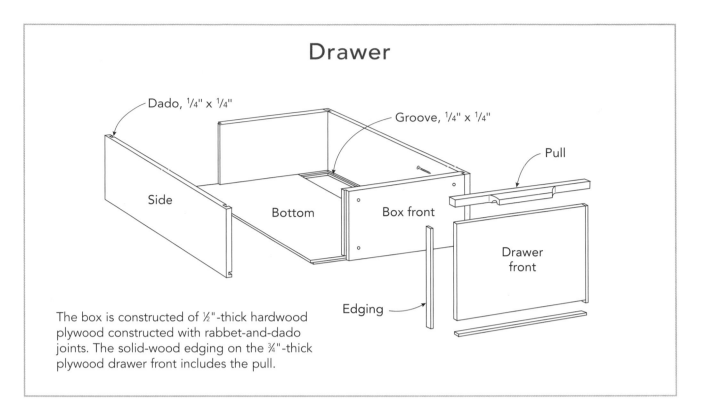

Drawer

Dado, ¼" x ¼"

Groove, ¼" x ¼"

Pull

Side

Bottom

Box front

Drawer front

Edging

The box is constructed of ½"-thick hardwood plywood constructed with rabbet-and-dado joints. The solid-wood edging on the ¾"-thick plywood drawer front includes the pull.

PHOTO C: Use hardwood cauls to distribute clamping pressure along the joints. Compare diagonal measurements to make sure the drawer box is square under clamp pressure. Cock the clamps a bit if necessary.

5. Lay out the shape of the pull on its blank (see "Drawer Pull" on p. 78). Then bandsaw to within 1⁄16 in. of the cut line.

6. Rout, file, or sand to the cut line. I like template routing for this because of its accuracy and repeatability (see **photo D** on p. 78). I make the template from ½-in.-thick hardwood plywood, cutting the shape with a jigsaw and then refining it with files and sandpaper.

7. Rout the recess on the underside of the pull using a ½-in.-diameter corebox bit mounted in the router table.

8. Glue each pull to its drawer front. After the glue cures, scrape the edging flush to the drawer front, feathering back from the projecting area of the pull.

9. Tilt the table-saw blade about 14 degrees and rip the bevel on the pull, with the drawer front lying on its back on the saw. The rear edge of the bevel should meet the plane of the drawer front after smoothing, so saw a bit shy of the final shape.

10. Smooth the bevel with a block plane; then sand the pull through 220 grit.

QUICK 'N' EASY DRAWER JOINTS

Here's a simple, accurate way to make drawers on the table saw from ½-in.-thick plywood. This approach requires minimal saw setup and creates strong drawers with tight joints. All you need is a good-quality dado head that cuts dadoes with clean walls and flat bottoms. The ¼-in.-wide dadoes will be made using only the two outer dado blades, with no chippers in between them.

1. Stand a piece of drawer stock against the rip fence and adjust the fence until the outer dado blade is flush to the outer face of the stock. Then raise the dado blade a bit shy of ¼ in., make a test cut, and measure it. Creep up on the depth of cut until ¼ in. of plywood thickness remains. Leave the blade at this height for all of the joint cuts.

2. Saw the dadoes in the drawer sides. Using the same saw setup, cut the bottom grooves in the sides and in the front and back pieces. Press the workpiece firmly downward and against the fence (see photo at top right).

3. Re-adjust the rip fence and cut the rabbets in the drawer front and back. A featherboard clamped to the saw table holds the workpiece vertically against the fence (see photo at middle right).

4. Slide the rip fence about ¹⁄₆₄ in. toward the blade; then saw the rabbets in all four edges of the drawer bottom. The slight rip fence adjustment allows for an easy, sliding fit of the bottom into its grooves (see photo at bottom right).

When applying solid-wood edging, press it into a liberal coat of glue on the plywood edge, sliding it back a forth a bit to transfer the glue. Align the edging; then let the glue set up tack for a few minutes before clamping. This minimizes slippage during clamping.

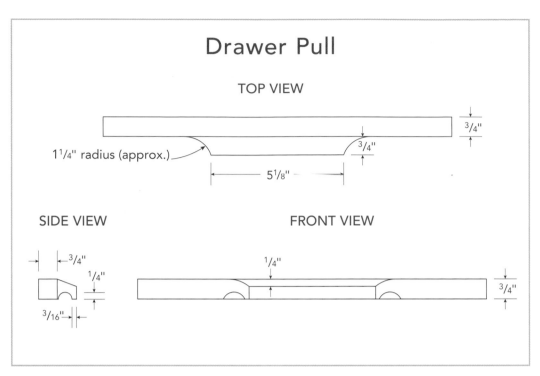

Drawer Pull

TOP VIEW

1¹/₄" radius (approx.)

5¹/₈"

³/₄"

³/₄"

SIDE VIEW

³/₄"

¹/₄"

³/₁₆"

FRONT VIEW

¹/₄"

³/₄"

PHOTO D: A template guides a flush-trimming bit for routing the pull to final shape. The wooden fence registers the pull blank and supports the router. Double-sided tape holds the blank to the template.

Installing the Drawers

Commercial drawer slides typically consist of two parts: One that attaches to the case and one that attaches to the drawer box. With the slides that I used, you mount the sliding rail assembly on the case and a quick-disconnect rail on the drawer box. If you use a different style of slide, refer to its installation instructions.

Attach the slides

1. Screw the drawer shims to the case sides. Align the bottom edge of each shim with the bottom of the drawer opening. The exposed faces of the shims must be flush to the face frame. Plane or shim them as necessary to accomplish this.

2. Screw each sliding rail assembly to its drawer shim. Make sure the slides are square to the face frame and set back ⅛ in. from it. Install just a front and a rear screw into the vertical slots for now.

3. Screw the rails to the drawer boxes. I used a 2¹⁵/₁₆-in.-wide spacer to locate each rail the proper distance from the bottom edge of the drawer side (see **photo E**).

4. Install the drawer boxes and adjust the slides as necessary to bring the drawer box front flush with the rear face of the face frame. There should be about ⅛ in. of space between the box bottom and the drawer opening.

Attach the drawer fronts and file rails

1. Remove the drawer boxes, and bore a ³⁄₁₆-in.-diameter hole through the box front near each lower inside corner (see "Drawer" on p. 76). Drill from the inside of the box.

2. Drill a ⁹⁄₆₄-in.-diameter hole through the box front near each top corner. Then countersink these holes from the inside of the box.

3. Reinstall the drawer boxes. Then apply a piece of thin double-sided tape to the outside of the drawer box front near each corner.

4. Place ¹⁄₁₆-in.-thick shims at the bottom of each drawer opening. Stand the drawer fronts on top of the shims and center them in their openings.

5. Press each drawer front firmly against the tape, then remove the drawers without shifting the fronts. Attach each drawer front using #6 by 1-in. pan-head screws driven through the ³⁄₁₆-in.-diameter lower holes.

6. Reinsert the drawers; then recheck the drawer opening gaps for consistency. If necessary, shift the drawer fronts using small bar clamps pulling against the drawer box on one end. When you're happy with the fit, drive a #6 by 1-in. drywall screw through each of the upper drawer box holes.

7. Replace the pan-head screws with drywall screws, countersinking the holes first. Any remaining inconsistencies in the gap can be corrected by handplaning the drawer edging.

8. Drive the rest of the screws into the drawer slides to secure the adjustments.

9. Cut the plastic file rails to length and snap them onto the drawer sides (see **photo F**).

Finishing Up

1. Touch-up sand all of the exposed surfaces. Then apply the finish of your choice. Sometimes I lacquer these cabinets, but I applied four coats of wiping varnish to this

PHOTO E: After installing the sliding rail assemblies to the case, attach the quick-disconnect rails to the drawer box sides. A plywood spacer quickly and accurately positions the rails.

one, sanding between coats with successively finer grits. (see "A Favorite Finish" on p. 19). Don't finish the drawer interiors unless you want to honestly complain about all of your "stinkin' bills."

2. Attach the cabinet top with six screws from inside.

PHOTO F: Plastic file rails slip tightly over the drawer sides to carry hanging file folders. No nails or screws are required.

CONVERTIBLE WINE CABINET

Unless you're an avowed wine collector, you don't need a wine cellar or huge cabinet dedicated to your prized fermentations. However, even the most modest of wine connoisseurs needs a way to store bottles on their sides to keep the corks swelled.

Many wine cabinets consist of X-shaped grids that support bottles lying on their sides. The problem with a grid design is that if your collection dwindles, you've got a lot of wasted space. Plus, a grid cabinet is very difficult to clean if wine is spilled or glass is broken inside.

This cherry wine cabinet, designed and built by professional cabinetmaker Adolph Schneider, solves both problems neatly. Wine bottles are cradled in racks that can be easily removed for cleaning or for temporary replacement with regular shelves when your wine supplies are low. The cabinet also includes racks for hanging wineglasses. This particular cabinet will accommodate nine bottles of wine without glasses, or six bottles with glasses. The cabinet shown in the drawings is a couple of inches taller than the one shown in the photo, to allow a bit more room for taller glasses.

Of course, you can make the cabinet any size you like—longer, wider, taller, whatever. Just follow the basic bottle spacing shown. Although most people like to display their wines, you could also make racks to fit inside your existing kitchen base cabinets.

CONVERTIBLE WINE CABINET

The hardwood plywood case is joined with splined miters; then the plywood edges are covered with veneer tape. The solid-wood bottle racks are joined with screwed and glued rabbets. The wineglass rails are attached with screws after finishing.

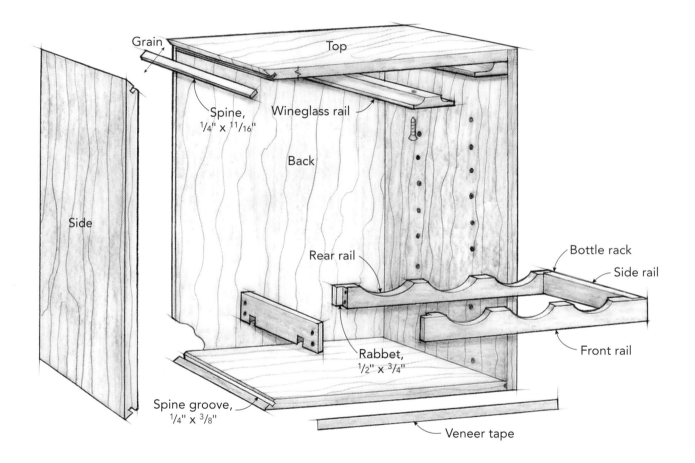

Grain

Top

Spine,
1/4" x 11/16"

Wineglass rail

Back

Side

Bottle rack

Side rail

Rear rail

Rabbet,
1/2" x 3/4"

Front rail

Spine groove,
1/4" x 3/8"

Veneer tape

DESIGN OPTIONS

✦ Make the wine cabinet case to match existing kitchen cabinetry; then modify the wall cabinets to accommodate the wine cabinet.

✦ Make a dedicated base cabinet with wine racks and standard shelves.

Side and Front Views

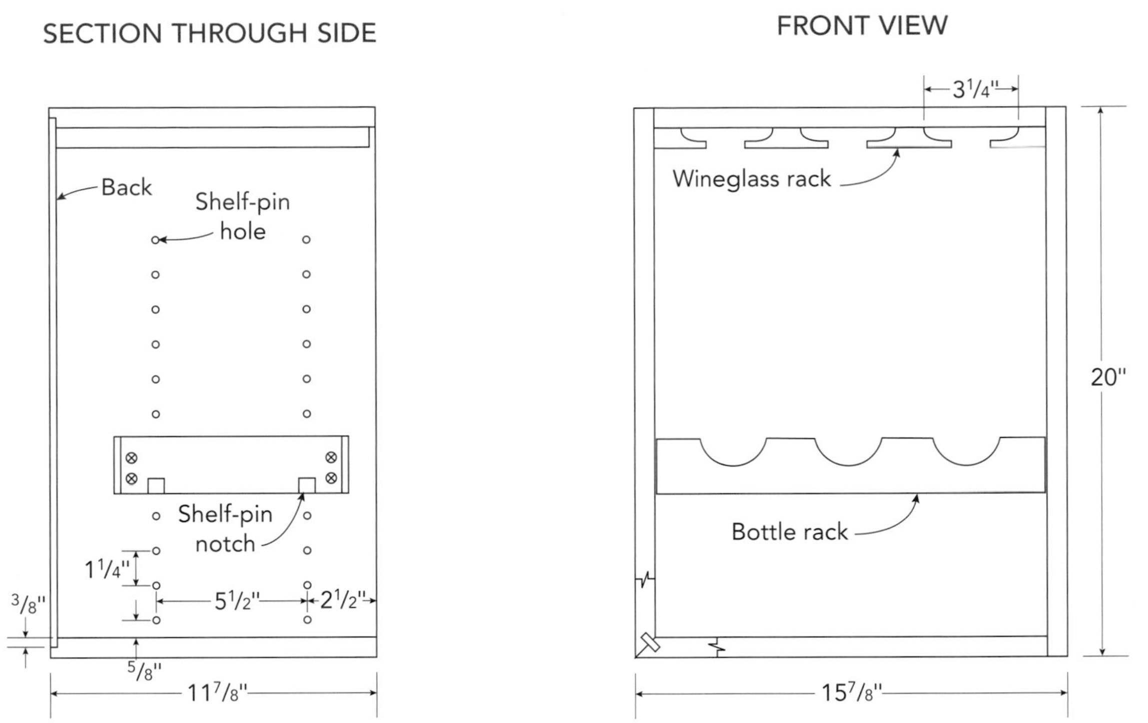

SECTION THROUGH SIDE

Back

Shelf-pin hole

Shelf-pin notch

$1^{1}/_{4}$"

$^{3}/_{8}$"

$5^{1}/_{2}$"

$2^{1}/_{2}$"

$^{5}/_{8}$"

$11^{7}/_{8}$"

FRONT VIEW

$3^{1}/_{4}$"

Wineglass rack

20"

Bottle rack

$15^{7}/_{8}$"

THIS CASE IS MADE from hardwood plywood that's mitered at the corners and reinforced with splines. The raw plywood edge is covered by veneer tape that's applied after the case is assembled. The interior bottle racks and wineglass rails are fitted after the case is assembled. The wineglass rails are simply screwed in place and the adjustable racks fit over shelf supports.

Constructing the Case

Layout and joinery

If you're customizing the size of the case, first determine the case width based on the bottle layout of the racks. Allow 4¼ in. between bottle centers and 3 in. between the center of an end bottle and the end of the rack.

1. Lay out the case sides, top, and bottom pieces end to end so that the grain will flow continuously around the top.

CUT LIST FOR WINE CABINET

Case

2	Sides	¾" x 11⅞" x 20"	hardwood plywood
2	Top/bottom	¾" x 11⅞" x 15⅞"	hardwood plywood
1	Back	¼" x 11⅛" x 15⅛"	hardwood plywood
	Veneer tape as needed		

Bottle rack

2	Side rails	¾" x 2" x 14⁵⁄₁₆"	solid wood
2	Front/rear rail	¾" x 2" x 8"	solid wood

Wineglass rack

2	Outer rails	¾" x 2⁵⁄₁₆" x 11⅜"	solid wood
2	Inner rails	¾" x 3" x 11⅜"	solid wood

Other materials

12	Shelf supports	from Woodworker's Hardware; item #WT8010

Parts for a single bottle rack.

Rack Layout

WINEGLASS RACK

FRONT VIEW

1"   1"   1/4"   1/2" radius

1 1/4"

BOTTLE RACK

SIDE VIEW

Screw

Shelf-pin notch

1/2"   1 1/4"

5 1/2"

5/8"   1 1/2"

BOTTOM VIEW

5/8"

Shelf-pin notch

1/8"

Side rail

FRONT RAIL

1 1/4" radius

1"

3"   4 3/16"

REAR RAIL

2" radius

1"

3"   4 3/16"

---

2. Saw the pieces to size using a good-quality blade to prevent grain tearout.

3. Miter both ends of the case sides, top, and bottom.

4. Rout a ¼-in.-wide by ⅜-in.-deep spline groove in each miter, favoring the inside edge of the miter. An easy way to do this is to clamp the pieces together and then use an edge guide to steer the router (see photo B on p. 38).

5. Saw a ¼-in. by ⅜-in. rabbet in the rear edge of each piece to accept the case back.

6. Make the ¼-in. by ¹¹⁄₁₆-in. splines. Good joint alignment depends on splines that fit snugly into their grooves. It's easiest to crosscut the splines from ¼-in.-thick construction plywood, sanding them if necessary for a good fit. Avoid hardwood plywood, which is typically thinner than its nominal size.

7. Dry-clamp the pieces together to check for good joint fit. You could use band clamps, but miter clamping cauls pull the joints together more neatly (see "Miter Clamping Cauls" on p. 40).

8. With the case still clamped up, cut the back to fit snugly within its rabbets.

Shelf-support holes and assembly

1. Disassemble the case and lay out the spacing for the shelf-support holes in the sides.

2. Drill the 5mm-diameter holes on the drill press; then sand the inside face of each piece through 220 grit.

3. Assemble the case, gluing only the corner joints for now. Place the back into its grooves unglued to hold the case square while the glue cures. Make sure the tips of the miters meet neatly.

4. Apply veneer tape to the front edges of the case; then sand it flush to the case sides.

5. Glue and nail the back into its rabbets. Wipe off any excess glue immediately.

6. Sand the outsides of the case through 220 grit. Be careful not to sand through the veneer, especially at the corners.

Constructing the Racks

Make the bottle racks

1. Plane and saw the rail pieces to size.

2. Lay out the arcs in the front and rear rails.

3. Saw the ½-in. by ¾-in. rabbets in the front and back rails that will accept the side rails.

4. Drill the arcs on the front rails using a 2½-in.-diameter hole saw on the drill press (see **photo A**).

5. Cut the arcs in the rear rails using a jigsaw or bandsaw.

6. Sand the arcs smooth. A large drum sander mounted on the drill press works well for this.

7. Slightly round over the inside edges of the front and back rails. Schneider uses a

⅛-in.-radius roundover bit set a bit shy of a complete quarter-round.

8. Drill and countersink the angled clearance holes for the screws that will hold the side rails in their rabbets (see **photo B** on p. 86).

9. Glue and screw the side rails into their rabbets using 1¼-in.-long screws in the upper holes to prevent the screws from projecting into the rear arcs. Use 1⅝-in.-long screws in the lower holes. If you need to drill a pilot first, make it small to prevent the screws from stripping out the end grain.

10. Lay out the shelf-support notches on the bottom edges of the side rails (see "Rack Layout").

PHOTO A: Use a hole saw to drill the arcs in the front rail of the bottle rack. Place the workpiece against a fence that sits ½ in. forward of the hole saw pilot bit.

PHOTO B: Drill and countersink clearance holes in the end rails of the bottle racks for attachment to the front rails. To angle the holes, rest the workpiece on a ³⁄₁₆-in.-thick shim set back 1¼ in. from the drill press fence.

PHOTO C: Schneider uses a ⅝-in.-diameter Forstner bit to drill the shelf-support notches in the undersides of the bottle rack side holes.

TIP

When drilling shelf-support holes, use a brad-point drill bit to minimize grain tearout.

11. Drill the shelf-support notches using a flat-bottom bit, such as a Forstner bit (see **photo C**).

12. Slightly round over all the remaining edges on the racks and sand the racks through 220 grit.

Make the wineglass racks

1. Plane and saw the rails to size.

2. Cut the cove profiles in the edges. Schneider used a molding head on the table saw, but you could rout the profile after wasting most of the cove on the table saw (see "Cutting the Wineglass Rack Rail Profile").

3. Drill and countersink two screw clearance holes in each rail for attachment to the case top.

4. Sand the rails through 220 grit.

Finishing Up

1. Touch-up sand the case and racks as necessary.

2. Apply an alcohol-resistant finish. This cabinet was finished with several coats of wiping varnish (see "A Favorite Finish" on p. 19).

3. Attach the wineglass rails with #6 by 1¼-in. screws (see **photo D**).

4. Fill cabinet with wine, and celebrate with a glass of Merlot.

Cutting the Wineglass Rack Rail Profile

Step 2.
Rout remainder
of cove.

Router table
fence

Step 1.
Waste bulk of
cove on table saw.

Wineglass rail
(end view)

Router table

½"-diameter corebox bit

PHOTO D: Screw the wineglass racks to the underside of the case top through predrilled countersunk clearance holes.

PANTRY DOOR SHELVES

ONE EXCELLENT AREA for storage is on the inside of a pantry door—a space that's often wasted. Here's a very simple set of shelves that you can screw to the door to hold everything from spices and canned goods to sandwich bags and aluminum foil.

What is ingenious about this design—presented to me by professional cabinetmaker Adolph Schneider—is the system of shelf stops. Each stop is simply a ¼-in.-diameter dowel that you bend to spring into its holes after assembling the unit. Schneider installs one dowel at the front of each shelf, but I decided to make a row of holes for each

dowel, so the stop can be moved in or out to accommodate larger or smaller items. When placed in the outermost holes, the stop will allow space for a typical 4-in.-diameter can. When placed in the other holes, the stop will prevent smaller canned goods or spice jars from shifting when the pantry door is opened.

The shelf cabinet is made of ½-in.-thick hardwood plywood edged with solid wood. The top and bottom fit into rabbets cut in the cabinet sides, and the shelves fit into dadoes. Solid-wood strips hide the edges of the plywood. Of course, you can size the cabinet to fit any door.

PANTRY DOOR SHELVES

The sides and top are made of ½"-thick hardwood plywood with solid-wood edging. The back is ¼"-thick hardwood plywood. The ¼"-diameter dowels are bent and sprung into their holes after the case is assembled.

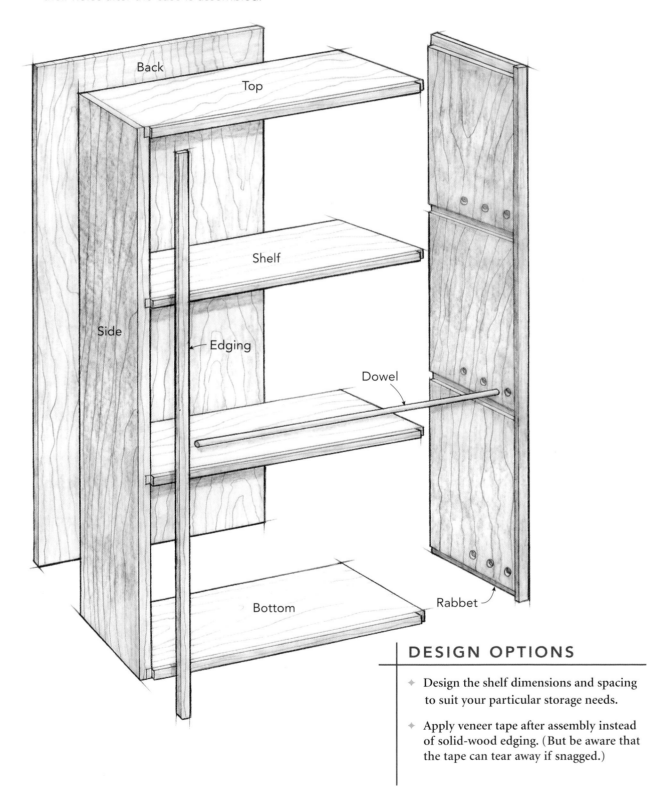

Back

Top

Shelf

Side

Edging

Dowel

Bottom

Rabbet

DESIGN OPTIONS

✦ Design the shelf dimensions and spacing to suit your particular storage needs.

✦ Apply veneer tape after assembly instead of solid-wood edging. (But be aware that the tape can tear away if snagged.)

Front and Side Views

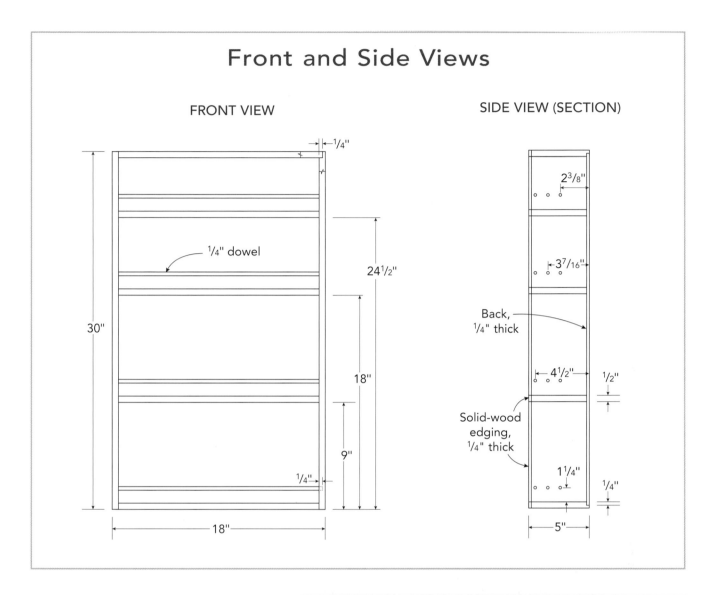

FRONT VIEW

SIDE VIEW (SECTION)

Y OU'LL BEGIN BY MAKING the parts and cutting the joints. After attaching the edging and drilling the dowel holes, you'll notch the ends of the top, bottom, and shelf edging and then assemble the case. After that, a quick sanding and a few coats of finish will complete the job.

Preparing the Parts and Joinery

Make the parts

1. Lay out the plywood and saw the sides, top, bottom, and shelves to size. Use a good-quality blade that won't tear the veneers when crosscutting and make sure to cut away any factory edges.

CUT LIST FOR PANTRY DOOR SHELVES

2	Sides	½" x 4¾" x 30"	hardwood plywood
2	Top/bottom	½" x 4¾" x 17½"	hardwood plywood
3	Shelves	½" x 4½" x 17½"	hardwood plywood
1	Back	¼" x 17½" x 29½"	hardwood plywood
4	Dowels	¼" diameter x 17⅜"	solid wood
2	Edging strips	¼" x ⁹⁄₁₆" x 30"	solid wood
5	Edging strips	¼" x ⁹⁄₁₆" x 17¼"	solid wood

PHOTO A:
Sandwich the solid-wood edging between its mating case pieces. Raise the case pieces on thin shims so the edging can overlap on both sides. Scrap strips protect the thin rear edges from clamp damage.

2. Make the ¼-in.-thick edging strips. I rip them from a board that I've planed to ⁵⁄₁₆ in. thick. I trim the overlap flush to the ½-in.-thick plywood after attaching the edging.

3. Saw the back, but leave it slightly oversize in length and width. You'll trim it for a perfect fit to its rabbets later.

Cut the joints

1. Lay out the dadoes for the shelves (see the drawing on p. 90). You'll probably want to customize the spacing to suit the size of your particular shelf cabinet, as well as the size of the items you plan to store in it. For aesthetic purposes, the sections should graduate from the largest at the bottom to the smallest at the top.

2. Mount a dado blade on your saw and shim it out to match the thickness of your plywood. Clamp an auxiliary fence to the rip fence; then saw the rabbets on the ends of the case sides (see photo A on p. 73). Alternatively, you could rout the rabbets as well as the shelf dadoes.

3. Using the rip fence as a stop, saw the dadoes to accept the shelves. Use a miter gauge with a long fence to guide the workpieces over the blade.

4. Saw or rout the ¼-in. by ¼-in. rabbets in the rear edges of the sides, top, and bottom, as shown in the drawing on p. 91.

Completing the Unit

Attach the edging and drill the holes

This cabinet has a lot of edging, which needs to be cut flush to the plywood pieces. Although you could apply the edging after assembling the case, routing or scraping it flush at the corners afterward can be difficult. As I'll show you here, you can attach the edging first; then notch it on the ends of the horizontal pieces, allowing them to tuck into the dadoes in the case sides.

1. Glue the edging onto all of the pieces, centering it across the thickness of the plywood. The shelf edging should extend to within about ⅛ in. of the end of the shelf. For efficiency, clamp two shelves together at once, keeping the edging in between (see **photo A**).

2. After the glue cures, plane the edging flush with the plywood. Alternatively, you could rout the edging flush using a flush-trimming bit first (see photo D on p. 134). Then plane or scrape it afterward.

3. Lay out the vertical spacing for the rows of ¼-in.-diameter by ¼-in.-deep dowel holes; then drill them on the drill press using a brad-point bit to prevent tearout. Use a fence to register each column of holes to the correct distance from the long edge of the workpiece.

4. Sand the pieces using a flat sanding block. Again, be careful not to round over the inside edges of the case pieces.

Notch the shelves and assemble the case

1. Trim the shelf edging to allow the ends of the top, bottom, and shelves to seat fully in the case dadoes. Using the table-saw rip fence as a stop, feed each shelf on edge, with the blade raised just shy of the plywood edge (see **photo B**).

2. Use a sharp chisel to remove any remaining glue or wood residue from the edge of the plywood at the notched section.

3. Dry-clamp the case to make sure that the joints all draw up tightly and that there are no gaps between the case and shelf edging. Make any necessary adjustments by trimming the shelves or edging.

4. With the case still dry-clamped, trim the back for a very snug fit in its rabbets.

5. Glue up the case, using cauls to distribute pressure evenly across the joints (see "Clamping Cauls" on p. 19). Insert the back unglued to help hold the case square, but check to make sure that the front edges are also square while under clamp pressure. Wipe away any excess glue immediately using a clean rag and clean water.

6. After the glue cures, re-sand as necessary to smooth any grain that was raised by clean-up water.

7. Glue and nail or glue and staple the back into its rabbets and let the glue cure thoroughly, as the back will be holding the cabinet to the pantry door.

Finishing Up

1. Sand the entire case through 220 grit, gently rounding the corners and front and rear edges.

PHOTO B: After gluing on the slightly long shelf edging, nip it off ¼ in. from the end. Use the rip fence as a stop.

PHOTO C: Spring the dowels into place by bending them enough to insert them into their holes.

2. Cut and sand the ¼-in.-diameter dowels and test-fit them in their holes (see **photo C**). The dowels should be about 7⁄16 in. longer than the distance between the inner faces of the case sides.

3. Apply a finish. This cabinet has several coats of an oil-varnish blend wiped on. (No need to get too fussy here; after all, it's inside a pantry most of the time.)

4. Hang the cabinet by screwing through the back in several places. If installing it on a hollow-core door, use molly or toggle bolts.

KITCHEN WORK STATION

IN MANY KITCHENS, counter space is at a premium. There just never seems to be enough, especially when you're cooking up a large or complicated dinner. That's when a portable kitchen work station can really come in handy. You can move it next to the stove or sink for an extra work area or for a staging platform for pots and dishes. The problem with many portable work stations is that they typically don't include much storage, so when they're not being used, they're basically wasting space.

I designed this oak mobile kitchen work station to satisfy the need for both extra counter space and extra storage. In smaller kitchens, you can roll it against a wall when you're not using it, and it's acts as a wall cabinet. In a larger kitchen, it can be left stationed in the center of the room where it will serve as an island. In fact, you can omit the casters if you don't intend to move the piece around much.

The cabinets underneath can be configured to suit your own needs. You can make all drawers, build a combination of drawers and closed cabinets, or incorporate open cabinets.

KITCHEN WORK STATION

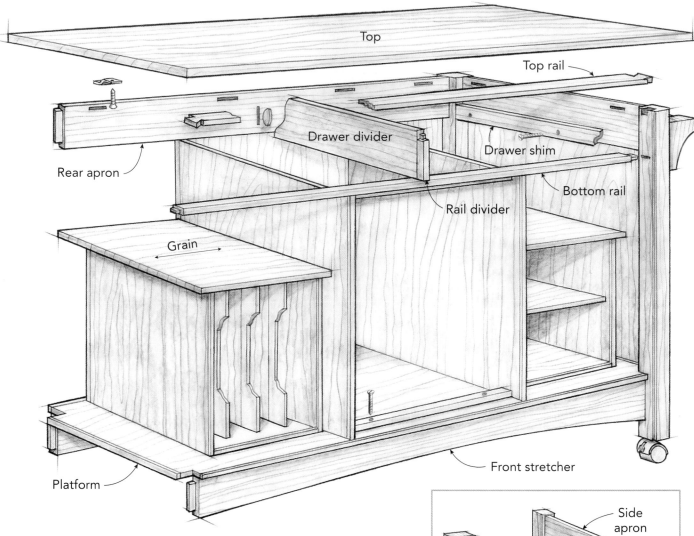

Top

Top rail

Drawer divider

Drawer shim

Rear apron

Bottom rail

Rail divider

Grain

Front stretcher

Platform

The work station consists of two basic components: the carriage and the cabinets. The carriage is the solid-wood framework of rails, aprons, stretchers, and platform that carries the cabinets. The plywood cabinets are built separately and then screwed to each other and to the carriage platform.

DESIGN OPTIONS

+ The top can be made from commercial butcher-block stock if desired.

+ The under-counter cabinets can be configured to suit your needs. (For example, the drawer cabinet can be replaced with open shelving or the cabinets can be faced with doors.)

+ For a permanent island, omit the casters and extend the leg length by 2½ in.

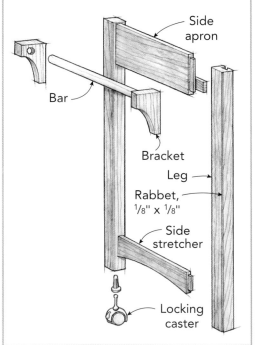

Side apron

Bar

Bracket

Leg

Rabbet, ⅛" x ⅛"

Side stretcher

Locking caster

Side and Front Views

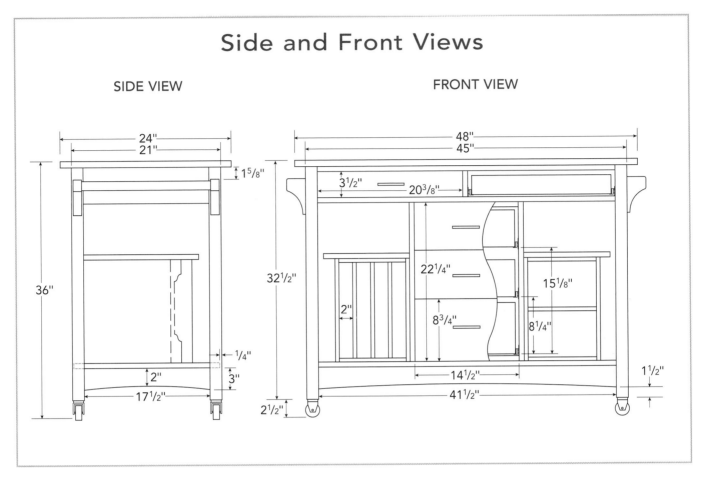

SIDE VIEW

FRONT VIEW

THE CARRIAGE is the framework of the work station and carries the top and cabinets. It consists of the legs, aprons, rails, and stretchers. I build it first and then construct the cabinets independently and install them underneath.

Constructing the Base Carriage and Tops

The kitchen work station uses a leg-and-apron framework that serves as a base for the three storage units that fit inside. There are also three tops: one on top of the unit and two smaller tops that fit over the lower storage compartments.

Make the tops

1. Using roughsawn 5/4 stock, lay out the boards for the 1-in.-thick top. Because the top will be prominent, take care to lay out the boards attractively (see "Composing

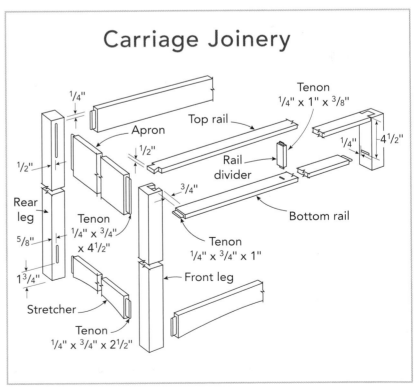

Carriage Joinery

CUT LIST FOR KITCHEN WORK STATION

Carriage

1	Top	1" x 24" x 48"	solid wood
4	Legs	1¾" x 1¾" x 32½"	solid wood
2	Side aprons	¾" x 5" x 19"	solid wood
1	Rear apron	¾" x 5" x 43"	solid wood
2	Side stretchers	¾" x 3" x 19"	solid wood
2	Front/ rear stretchers	¾" x 3" x 43"	solid wood
2	Rails	¾" x 1½" x 43"	solid wood
1	Rail divider	¾" x 1½" x 4¼"	solid wood
1	Drawer divider	¾" x 4¼" x 18¼"	hardwood plywood
1	Platform	¾" x 20" x 44"	hardwood plywood
2	Platform edgings	¼" x ¾" x 17½"	solid wood
2	Platform edgings	¼" x ¾" x 41½"	solid wood
4	Brackets	1¼" x 2¾" x 5"	solid wood
2	Bars	1¼" diameter x 19"	solid wood

Cabinets

2	Cabinet tops	¾" x 17¼" x 12"	solid wood
2	Drawer case sides	¾" x 18⅞" x 22¼"	hardwood plywood
1	Drawer case back	¾" x 14½" x 22¼"	hardwood plywood
2	Drawer case braces	¾" x 2½" x 14½"	solid wood
4	Small case sides	½" x 15½" x 14⅜"	hardwood plywood
2	Small case back	½" x 9½" x 14⅜"	hardwood plywood
4	Small case top/bottoms	½" x 15½" x 9½"	hardwood plywood
3	Small case dividers	½" x 12¾" x 13⅜"	hardwood plywood
1	Small cabinet shelf	½" x 15¼" x 9⅜"	hardwood plywood
2	Rear edgings	¾" x ¾" x 22¼"	solid wood

Cabinets

4	Rear edgings	½" x ½" x 14⅜"	solid wood
2	Front edgings	¼" x ¾" x 22¼"	solid wood
4	Front edgings	¼" x ½" x 14⅜"	solid wood
5	Front edgings	¼" x ½" x 9½"	solid wood
3	Divider edgings	½" x 1½" x 13⅜"	solid wood

Drawers

4	Drawer sides	½" x 2⅝" x 18"	solid wood
4	Drawer box front/backs	½" x 3" x 19⅜"	solid wood
2	Drawer bottoms	¼" x 18¼" x 18¾"	hardwood plywood
4	Drawer sides	½" x 5¼" x 18"	solid wood
2	Drawer sides	½" x 7¼" x 18"	solid wood
4	Drawer box front/backs	½" x 5¼" x 13½"	solid wood
2	Drawer box front/backs	½" x 7¼" x 13½"	solid wood
3	Drawer bottoms	¼" x 18¼" x 12⅞"	hardwood plywood
2	Drawer shims	¾" x 2" x 17½"	hardwood plywood
2	Drawer fronts	¾" x 3⁷⁄₁₆" x 20⁵⁄₁₆"	solid wood
2	Drawer fronts	¾" x 6¹¹⁄₁₆" x 14⅜"	solid wood
1	Drawer fronts	¾" x 8¹¹⁄₁₆" x 14⅜"	solid wood

Other materials

5 pair	Drawer slides	18"	*from* Woodworker's Hardware; item #RH501 18 ALM
5	Pulls	3"	*from* Woodworker's Hardware; item #A02378 PWT
4	Stem-type casters	2"	*from* Woodworker's Hardware; item #JH50 SBB
12	Metal tabletop fasteners		

Dimensions for all pieces with tenons include tenon length.

COMPOSING GRAIN FOR PANELS

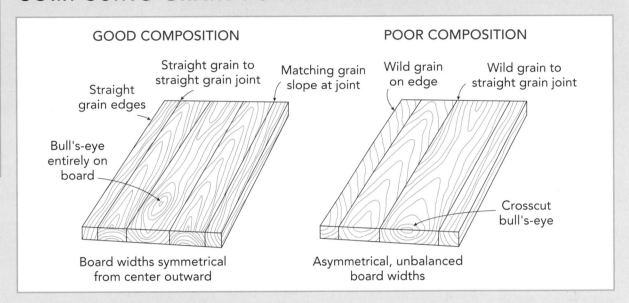

GOOD COMPOSITION

Straight grain edges

Straight grain to straight grain joint

Matching grain slope at joint

Bull's-eye entirely on board

Board widths symmetrical from center outward

POOR COMPOSITION

Wild grain on edge

Wild grain to straight grain joint

Crosscut bull's-eye

Asymmetrical, unbalanced board widths

Thoughtful board layout can make all the difference in the look of a solid-wood panel. When laying out, use long boards, sliding them against each other to create a good match at the joints. The tips shown above are just guidelines, of course. Rip, flip, and arrange the boards in whatever way is necessary to create the most continuous grain pattern and consistent color.

Grain for Panels"). While you're at it, join up the cabinet tops.

2. Joint and thickness plane the boards; then edge-join them together.

3. Plane or belt sand the tops. If you have access to a wide belt or drum sander, this is the perfect application for it (see **photo A**).

4. Round over the edges with a ⅛-in.-radius roundover bit or a handplane and sandpaper. Don't round over the edges of the cabinet tops that abut the center cabinet.

Prepare the parts

1. Lay out the stock for the parts. I used straight-grained material for the legs, ripping the pieces from the outer edges of wide 8/4 plainsawn boards.

2. Joint, plane, and rip the pieces straight and square; then crosscut them to length.

PHOTO A: A wide drum sander is the perfect tool for sanding tops. It quickly creates a smooth, flat surface.

PHOTO B: When routing the leg mortises, plunge to full depth at the mortise ends; then remove the remaining waste, taking shallow passes.

PHOTO C: A shoulder plane makes neat work of trimming tenon shoulders.

Cut the joints

1. Mark the legs for orientation; then lay out the leg mortises for the aprons and stretchers. Notice that the stretcher mortises are set in ⅛ in. more than are the apron mortises.

2. Rout the mortises using an edge guide on your router (see **photo B**).

3. Lay out and rout the mortises for the bottom rail and the rail divider. I use a shop-made T-square to guide the router (see photo A on p. 38).

4. Rout the ⅛-in. by ⅛-in. rabbets in the three outer edges of each leg.

5. Saw the apron and stretcher tenons. I cut them on the table saw using a dado head. Aim for a snug fit in the mortises and against the leg. If necessary, trim the tenons with a rabbet or with a shoulder plane (see **photo C**).

6. Saw the rail and rail divider tenons for a snug fit in their mortises.

7. Lay out the stretcher curves. You can either use a long trammel bar as a compass or you can trace along a thin strip of wood pulled to the proper curvature (see "Springing a Curve").

8. Cut the stretcher curves with a bandsaw or jigsaw; then clean up the saw marks with a spokeshave, files, and sandpaper.

9. Dry-assemble the bottom rail and front stretcher to the front legs. Then lay out the dovetails on the top rail. I use a 7-degree angle on the dovetails and mark the shoulders directly from the legs.

10. Saw the dovetails; then trace their shapes onto the tops of the front legs using a sharp pencil. Align the rear of the rail with the inner faces of the legs. I rout out the dovetail sockets just shy of my cut lines and then pare to them with a sharp chisel.

11. Make the plywood drawer divider, glue it to the rail divider, and cut the biscuit slots for joining its rear edge to the rear apron, as shown in the drawing on p. 96.

12. Sand all carriage parts through 220 grit. Round over the edges of the leg rabbets slightly, but don't sand the innermost edges of the legs until after fitting the platform.

Make the platform and assemble the carriage

1. Dry-clamp the carriage to make sure the joints all pull up tight and align properly.

2. Glue up the side assemblies, making sure that the legs, aprons, and stretchers lie flat and square to each other under clamp pressure.

3. Make the platform edging pieces, cutting them slightly oversize. Then glue them to the platform, centering each one on the edge. Then plane, scrape, or sand the edging flush to the plywood.

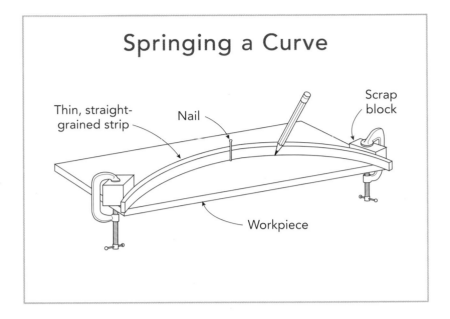

Springing a Curve

Thin, straight-grained strip

Nail

Scrap block

Workpiece

TIP

When wiping away excess glue, use a clean rag and replenish your water often to avoid spreading diluted glue into the wood grain. Alternatively, you can wait until the excess glue turns rubbery and then trim it off with a sharp chisel.

PHOTO D: After jigsawing the platform notches just a hair small, pare them to final size, guiding a chisel against a square wooden block.

PHOTO E: After gluing up the two side assemblies and notching the platform, glue and insert the rear apron, lower rail, and stretchers to one side assembly. Then slip one end of the platform unglued between the legs, and glue on the opposite side assembly.

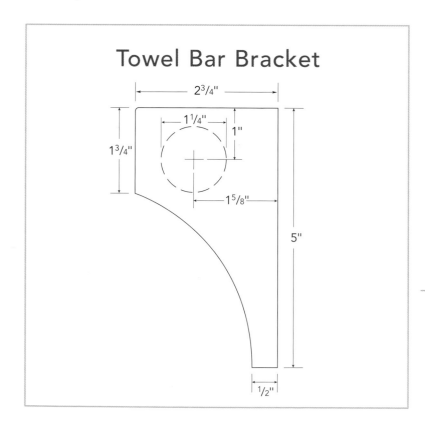

Towel Bar Bracket

2³/₄"

1¹/₄"

1"

1³/₄"

1⁵/₈"

5"

¹/₂"

4. Dry-clamp the bottom rail, rear apron, and stretchers to the side assemblies. Measure the distances between the legs; then mark out the platform notches, carefully measuring outward from the center of the platform. Aim for a very snug fit between the legs.

5. Cut the notches. For the best fit, saw them slightly undersize and then pare them to your cut line (see **photo D** on p. 101). When you've got a good fit, sand the platform through 220 grit.

6. Glue the bottom rail, rear apron, and stretchers to the side assemblies (see **photo E**). Make sure the apron is lined up with the tops of the legs and that the stretchers are spaced 1½ in. up from the bottoms of the legs. Raise the platform off the stretchers to prevent glue squeeze-out from touching it.

7. After removing the clamps, run a thin bead of glue along the top edges of the stretchers; then clamp the platform down.

8. Glue and clamp the rail divider and top rail into place.

9. Sand the innermost corner of each leg, rounding it slightly with 150 grit and then 220 grit.

10. Drill the holes for the caster posts. To guide your bit, use a block that you've pre-bored on the drill press and then clamped to the leg. The casters I used required a ²⁹/₆₄-in.-diameter hole, but first drill a test hole in scrap to be sure.

Make the bar assembly

If you're not equipped to turn your own bars, you can order commercial dowel stock. I got mine from Woodworker's Supply (see "Sources" on p. 172).

1. Make the blanks for the bar brackets.

TIP

To prevent marring your workpieces, glue thick leather scraps to the faces of pipe clamps using contact cement.

Cabinets

The cabinets are built of hardwood plywood panels edged with solid wood, which is applied to all front edges and to the rear edges of the sides. Then the pieces are joined with biscuits to ease alignment. Drawers are installed with commercial drawer slides.

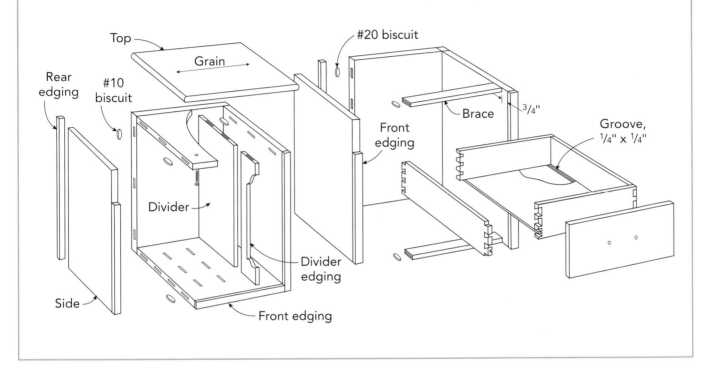

Building the Cabinets

Size the parts and cut the joints

1. Lay out the case pieces and cut them to size. Make sure the drawer case sides and back will slip between the platform and the rail and apron with just a bit of room to spare.

2. Mill the solid-wood edging, ripping it from stock that you've planed about ¹⁄₃₂ in. thicker than the plywood. The edging at the rear of each cabinet is square in cross section, whereas the edging at the front is ¼ in. thick (see "Cabinets").

3. Make the edging pieces. Cut each one slightly longer than the edge to be covered.

4. Glue the edging to the case sides, tops, bottoms, and dividers. Make sure that it overlaps the plywood on the ends and both faces.

5. Plane, scrape, or sand the edging flush to the plywood faces. Then trim it flush at the

2. Make a stiff paper pattern of the bracket (see "Towel Bar Bracket"). Then trace the shape onto the blanks.

3. Using a Forstner or other flat-bottom bit in a drill press, bore the ½-in.-deep blind holes to accept the bar. If your dowel stock is ¹⁄₁₆ in. or more undersize (mine was), use a smaller diameter bit. Clamp the bracket blanks to a fence to secure them while drilling.

4. Bandsaw the brackets to shape, sawing just outside of the cut line. Save the offcuts.

5. Sand to the cut line to smooth the curve. I used an oscillating spindle sander, but a regular drum sander in a drill press would work.

6. Cut the bars to length and insert them into their holes. If a dowel is slightly oversize, trim down the diameter with a block plane. Then sand the bars and brackets through 220 grit and set them aside for now.

> **TIP**
>
> Manila folders make great material for small patterns. The paper is thin enough to cut easily but thick and stiff enough to trace around.

PHOTO F: Trim the edging flush to the case pieces by aligning a shim block flush with the outside face of the saw-blade teeth.

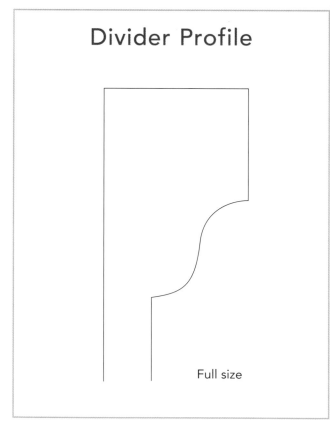

Divider Profile

Full size

ends. I do this on the table saw using a shim block clamped to the fence (see **photo F**).

6. Make a thick paper pattern of the ogee profile for the divider fronts (see "Divider Profile"). Then trace the profile onto the divider edging.

7. Saw the profile. I cut the curved sections with a scrollsaw and the straight sections with a bandsaw. Clean up the straight sections with a block plane, chisel, and sandpaper.

8. Make the braces for the center cabinet and drill the shelf support holes in the sides of the right-hand cabinet.

9. Lay out the biscuit joints for joining the case pieces, including the dividers. The small cabinets take #10 biscuits and the center cabinet takes #20 biscuits.

10. Cut the biscuit joints. When cutting slots into the face of a panel at the edge, clamp scrap to the panel for joiner fence support (see **photo G**). When cutting the divider slots, prop the divider up on ⅛-in.-thick shims to center the slots (see **photo H**).

PHOTO G: Square scrap clamped to the case pieces provides bearing for the biscuit joiner fence, preventing angled slots.

PHOTO H: When cutting biscuit joints for ½-in.-thick dividers, lay the divider on ⅛-in.-thick shims to center the slot in the end of the divider. To use the divider as a fence for cutting the case bottom slots, as shown here, use a ⅛-in.-thick spacer to offset the divider from the joint intersection line.

PHOTO I: To attach the bar brackets, set them on a length of thick scrap clamped to the legs. Clamp the lower section of each bracket using the curved offcuts. Thick leather scraps protect the finish.

the back, then the sides. Make sure all the cabinets are square under clamp pressure.

4. Finish-sand all surfaces that will be exposed.

5. Because of oak's open grain, I next treated the carriage and cabinets with pore filler to ensure a smoother finish. I also installed the case-half of each slide. It's easiest to do all this before installing the cabinets.

6. Fit the drawer shims to the carriage and screw them in place, as shown in the drawing on p. 96. Then install the drawer slides into the carriage.

Install the bars and cabinets

1. Spot-glue the bars into their brackets, orienting the annular rings on the ends of the bars parallel to the grain of the brackets to ensure equal wood movement. Then glue the brackets to the carriage legs (see **photo I**).

2. Install the center cabinet, insetting it ½ in. from the rear edge of the platform. I screwed through the bottom braces into the platform and then into the cabinet sides from underneath. Next, square up the face of the cabinet and shim any space between the sides and the bottom rail, making sure that the rails are square to the legs. Then screw through the rail into the sides (see **photo J**).

3. Install the small cabinets, insetting them ½ in. from the rear edge of the platform. Screw through the center cabinet sides into the top edges of the small cabinets, and through the platform into the cabinet sides.

Making the Drawers

Build the boxes

I made the drawer boxes from solid poplar, dovetailing the corners. Alternatively, you could use ½-in.-thick plywood, joining the corners with rabbet-and-dado joints (see "Quick 'n' Easy Drawers" on p. 77). If doing the latter, simply subtract ½ in. from the given lengths of the drawer box fronts and backs.

Assemble the cabinets

1. Sand the dividers and the inside faces of the small cabinets, being careful not to round over the edges.

2. The divider cabinet would be difficult to finish after assembly, so mask off the joints and finish the dividers and inside faces of the case pieces now. While you're at it, finish the bars and exposed faces of the brackets too, as it'll be difficult to brush a finish onto them once they're attached. Leave about ⅜ in. of raw wood at the ends of the bars for gluing later.

3. Glue up all three cabinets. When assembling the divider cabinet, I first glue the dividers to the top and bottom, using deep-throat clamps at the center. Next, I attach

1. Plane, rip, and crosscut the drawer box pieces to size.

2. Saw the bottom grooves in the sides and box fronts, as shown in "Cabinets" on p. 103.

3. Cut the drawer box corner joints (see "Dovetailed Drawer Construction" on p. 113).

4. Assemble the drawers on a flat surface and compare the diagonals to ensure that the boxes are square under clamp pressure.

5. Sand the drawer boxes and ease the edges and corners with 150-grit sandpaper.

6. Attach the drawer slides to the drawer boxes; then fit them into the case, making sure that the drawer box fronts are parallel to the front of the case and carriage.

Fit the drawer fronts

1. Make the drawer fronts, initially sizing them to the drawer openings; then set them in place.

2. Using a pencil and ruler, draw a cut line around the edge of each drawer front to create a gap of about $\frac{3}{32}$ in. all around. Then saw and plane to the cut line. Check the fit of the fronts and then remove all of the drawers except the bottom one.

3. Loosely clamp the drawer front to the bottom drawer box. Shift the front to achieve an even gap all around; then clamp the front tightly, remove the drawer, and screw the front on from inside the drawer. Repeat the procedure for the next drawer up.

4. Because there's no clamp access for the top drawer in the cabinet, use double-sided tape to hold the drawer front in place before screwing it on.

5. Use deep throat clamps to hold the drawer fronts to the two carriage drawers; then screw the fronts on with the drawers in place.

Finishing Up

1. Apply finish to all exposed surfaces. I brushed on two coats of semigloss polyurethane, wet-sanding with 400-grit sandpaper between coats. I sanded the final coat with 600-grit sandpaper to remove any nibs and then scrubbed it with 0000 steel wool to reduce the gloss somewhat.

2. Screw on the cabinet tops, aligning the rear edge of each with the rear edge of the center cabinet. Because a drill won't fit into the rear of the divider cabinet, I glued the rear portion of the top to the cabinet top. Elongate the front screw holes to allow about $\frac{3}{8}$ in. wood movement.

3. Using a biscuit joiner or slot-cutting router bit, cut the slots in the aprons and rails to accept tabletop clips.

4. Attach the work station top. I used commercial S-shaped metal fasteners, setting them at least $\frac{1}{8}$ in. away from the rail and rear apron to allow for wood movement.

5. Attach the pulls.

PHOTO J: After shimming any space between the lower rail and the cabinet sides, drill a screw clearance hole through the rail and shims. Countersink the holes; then screw the rails to the cabinet sides.

BED PEDESTAL

ALMOST EVERYONE stashes things under the bed, particularly large items. But if you were to peek under the typical bed, you would find a jumble of stuff, usually shoved together in a dusty pile. Some solutions for under-bed storage include using cardboard boxes or roll-out trays. But these are only partial fixes, as boxes need to be pulled entirely out to be opened, and most roll-out trays don't have lids to keep out dust.

Professional woodworker Ken Burton designed and built a bed platform that solves these problems. The platform consists of a pair of drawer cases that serve as a pedestal for his queen-size bed. The drawers provide clean storage with quick access,

and the space between the two cases creates a cavity for stashing long objects like skis, fishing poles, and bolts of fabric. Each case contains three large drawers joined at the corners with dovetails for great strength. A cavity at one end of the case allows access for bolting a headboard to the cases.

Burton used ¾-in.-thick fir AC-grade construction plywood for his cases because it's less expensive than hardwood plywood. The plywood shows only at the foot of an undraped bed. If you like, you can cover it there with veneer or more attractive panels. Burton's drawer fronts are walnut, but of course you can use any wood.

BED PEDESTAL

The twin cases are made from ¾"-thick plywood joined with glue and screws, using biscuits for easy alignment. The plywood edges around the drawer openings are covered with ¼"-thick solid-wood strips. The drawers are joined with through dovetails at the rear and half-blind dovetails at the front.

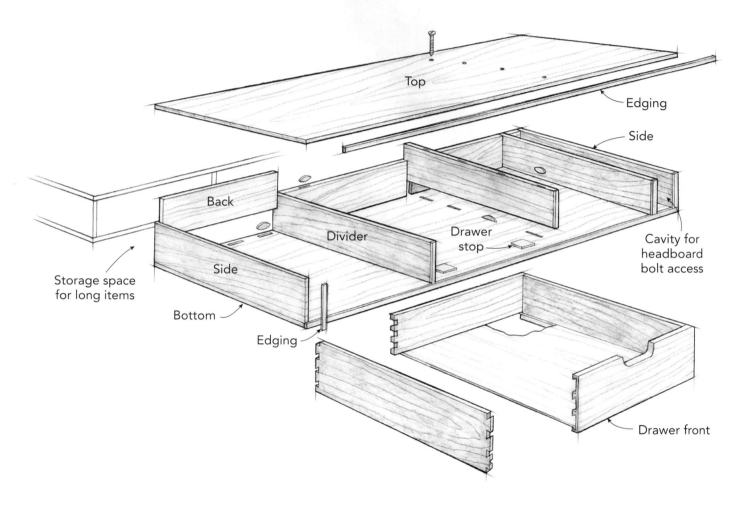

Top

Edging

Side

Back

Divider

Drawer stop

Cavity for headboard bolt access

Side

Storage space for long items

Bottom

Edging

Drawer front

DESIGN OPTIONS

◆ If the box springs are omitted, the drawers can be made deeper or stacked two high.

◆ A single case can be made to suit a twin bed mattress set.

◆ The drawers can be reduced in width by 1 in. and mounted on commercial slides.

◆ The headboard bolt cavity can be covered with a removable panel or omitted if no headboard is desired.

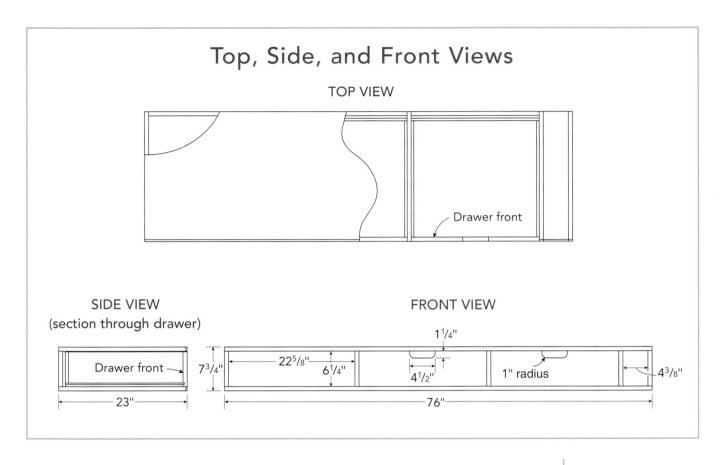

Top, Side, and Front Views

TOP VIEW

SIDE VIEW
(section through drawer)

Drawer front

7³/₄"

23"

FRONT VIEW

Drawer front

1¹/₄"

22⁵/₈"

6¹/₄"

4¹/₂"

1" radius

4³/₈"

76"

THE PEDESTAL CONSISTS simply of the cases and the drawers. The cases, which are easy to build, are made first. Then the drawers are constructed and fit to their openings.

Making the Case

Cut the pieces and apply the edging

1. Lay out the plywood pieces.
2. Cut the pieces to size. Rip the back pieces to width, but crosscut them about ⅛ in. oversize in length for now.
3. Mill the edging, ripping the strips from a ¹³/₁₆-in.-thick board. Crosscut each strip slightly longer than the edge to be covered.
4. Glue the edging to the pieces.
5. Scrape or sand the edging flush to the panels; then trim the ends flush (see photo F on p. 104).

Assemble the case

1. Lay out the biscuit joints on the inside faces of the top and bottom panels and on the top and bottom edges of the sides, dividers, and backs.
2. Cut the biscuit slots.
3. Dry-fit the sides and dividers between the top and bottom panels; then cut the backs to fit exactly into their openings. A good fit here will help keep the case square for a good drawer fit.
4. Test-fit the backs and double-check the entire case for good joint fits.
5. Glue and screw the case together, making sure that everything is as square as possible before driving the screws home. Wipe up any excess glue immediately with a clean, wet rag.

Making the Drawers

For the best fit, size the drawers to fit the height of their openings exactly; then hand-plane them for a snug but easy sliding fit after assembly. Dovetails are the best joint

TIP

When gluing edging strips to similarly sized panels, clamp up the panels in pairs with the strips in the center. The panels themselves will serve as clamping cauls to provide even pressure across the strips.

Case

2	Top/bottom	¾" x 22¾" x 76"	plywood
5	Dividers	¾" x 6¼" x 22½"	plywood
3	Backs	¾" x 6¼" x 22⅝"	plywood
	Edging stock	¼" x ¾" x 16'	solid wood

Drawers

3	Fronts	¾" x 6¼" x 22⅝"	solid wood
3	Backs	⁹⁄₁₆" x 5⁵⁄₁₆" x 22⅝"	solid wood
6	Sides	⁹⁄₁₆" x 6¼" x 20¼"	solid wood
3	Bottoms	¼" x 20" x 21⅞"	hardwood plywood

Case parts are for one unit; drawer parts are for one case.

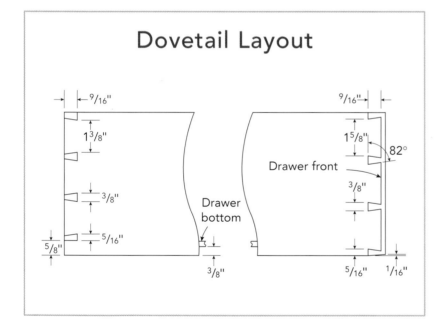

Dovetail Layout

to use for large heavy drawers because they can withstand strong pulling forces. However, if you don't feel like tackling dovetails, you could use rabbet-and-dado joints with applied drawer fronts (see the instructions for the file cabinet on p. 68).

Prepare the stock

1. Mill stock for the drawer fronts. If possible, use one long board for each run of adjacent drawer fronts.

2. Lay out the drawer fronts, noting their sequence for continuous grain orientation in the case later.

3. Mill stock for the sides and backs.

4. Rip all of the pieces to width, taking measurements directly from the drawer openings. Rip the drawer fronts and sides to exactly the height of the openings. Rip the drawer backs ⅝ in. less than that.

5. Crosscut the pieces to length, making each drawer front and its matching back ³⁄₃₂ in. less than the width of their drawer opening.

Cut the dovetails

These drawers use half-blind dovetails for the fronts and through dovetails for the drawer backs. Although we're using a hand dovetail technique here, you could also use one of the many popular router jigs for this operation.

1. Saw the ¼-in.-deep drawer bottom grooves in the front and sides. The grooves sit ⅜ in. up from the bottom edges.

2. Set a marking gauge to the thickness of the drawer side; then use it to scribe the dovetail-pin baseline across both faces of each pin board and tail board. Also scribe across the edges of the tail boards.

3. Using a bevel gauge set to about 82 degrees, lay out the angle of the pins with a sharp pencil (see **photo A**).

4. Saw the pins, staying to the waste side of the lines. A fine-tooth saw that cuts cleanly and tracks well makes all the difference when sawing dovetails. Lines extending from the workpiece edge to the scribed baseline help guide your cut (see **photo B**).

5. To remove the waste, begin by tapping just outside the baseline with a sharp chisel. With the bevel side of the chisel facing toward the end of the board, the force of the mallet will drive the chisel backward to the baseline.

6. Lean the chisel steeply and make a light V-cut back to the baseline to establish a shoulder for registering subsequent baseline cuts (see **photo C** on p. 114).

7. Deepen the baseline cut, angling the chisel just a bit to create a slight undercut

Dovetailed Drawer Construction

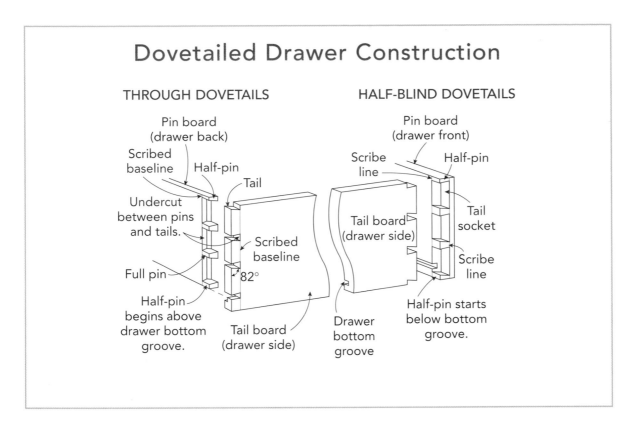

THROUGH DOVETAILS

Pin board (drawer back)
Scribed baseline
Half-pin
Tail
Undercut between pins and tails.
Scribed baseline
82°
Full pin
Half-pin begins above drawer bottom groove.
Tail board (drawer side)

HALF-BLIND DOVETAILS

Pin board (drawer front)
Scribe line
Half-pin
Tail board (drawer side)
Tail socket
Scribe line
Drawer bottom groove
Half-pin starts below bottom groove.

PHOTO A: Lay out the dovetail pins first, setting the bevel gauge to about 82 degrees.

PHOTO B: Saw down carefully to the scribed baseline, keeping the saw vertical.

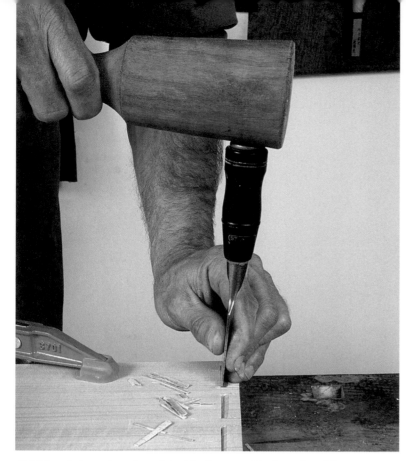

PHOTO C: Leaning the chisel helps establish a shoulder for the cuts.

of the shoulder, which will help the joints close tightly.

8. Chisel backward at a steep angle to remove more waste. Make subsequent cuts in the same manner—first at the shoulder, then at a steep backward angle to remove the waste. Repeat until you're halfway through the workpiece.

9. Flip the workpiece over and chop away the remainder of the waste from the other side, working in the same way (see **photo D**).

10. Clean out any chips in the corners using a sharp knife.

11. Stand the pin board on the tail board and trace around the pins. Use a sharp pencil or knife, pulling it toward the wide face of the pins. Afterward, extend the lines across the end of the workpiece to help you cut squarely (see **photo E**).

12. To cut the tails, keep the sawblade to the waste side of a cut line, splitting it in half. Avoid cutting the tails so fat that you have to chisel them for a good fit—a very time-consuming practice.

13. Chisel away the waste between the tails as you did for the pins, again undercutting

PHOTO D: After chopping halfway through the pin board, flip it over and remove the remaining waste from the opposite side.

PHOTO E: The tails are marked from the completed pins. Afterward, layout lines are extended squarely across the end of the tail board.

at the shoulder. Take care not to dig into the tails when leaning the chisel over (see **photo F**).

14. Saw away the waste at the edges, again splitting the line.

15. To lay out the half-blind pins, first set a marking gauge to the thickness of a drawer side; then scribe the inside face and edge of the drawer front (see **photo G.**)

16. After laying out the pins, saw as much of their cheeks as possible by angling the saw between the two scribed lines. Notice that the lower half-pin lies outside the drawer bottom groove (see **photo H** on p. 116).

17. Use a thin, unburnished scraper to deepen the cut, but be careful not to split the workpiece, especially if it's a hard wood. This technique works best with softer woods like poplar and pine (see **photo I** on p. 116).

18. After chiseling out the bulk of the waste, flatten the bottom of the tail socket down to the scribed line (see **photo J** on p. 117).

19. Stand the pin board on the tail board, aligning the bottom of the tail sockets with the end of the tail board; then trace the pins. Saw and chop the tails as before.

PHOTO F: Remove the waste between the tails, taking care not to dig into the crisp edges.

PHOTO G: With a marking gauge, scribe the inside faces and ends of the drawer fronts to begin layout of the half-blind dovetails.

PHOTO H: A saw starts the half-blind dovetail pins with an angled cut that joins the two layout lines.

Finish and assemble the drawers

1. Lay out the handholds. Then drill the ends of the cutouts on the drill press (see **photo K**).

2. Cut the straight bottom section of each handhold with a jigsaw or bandsaw; then sand the profile smooth with a drum sander. Rout both the inside and outside edges with a ¼-in.-diameter roundover bit to soften the feel.

3. Dry-assemble the drawers. Then cut the drawer bottoms to fit snugly between their grooves.

4. Glue up the drawers. If your joints were cut well, you shouldn't need to use clamps. However, if you need to clamp the joints, use cauls placed directly over the tails, with slots cut on the underside to span the pins (see "Dovetail Cauls"). Insert the drawer bottoms to keep the drawers square while the glue dries.

5. Screw each drawer bottom to the bottom edge of its drawer back.

Fit the drawers

1. Plane any saw marks off the top and bottom edge of each drawer; then lay the drawer on a flat surface to check for any

PHOTO I: Gently tap a scraper into the established kerf to finish the cut.

rocking. Plane the bottom if necessary to make the drawer rest flat.

2. Check the fit of each drawer in its opening. Plane the top edges until you've got an easy, sliding fit in the opening. If you're doing this during the humid summer season, leave the fit fairly tight. If you're working during the dry winter months, plane off a bit more to prevent the drawers from sticking when they swell during summertime.

3. Plane or sand the edges of the drawer front until you achieve an even gap of about ¹⁄₁₆ in. all around the drawer. Because of the drawer sides, the bottom edge of the drawer front would be difficult plane squarely. Instead, plane it at an angle to create a gap at the front (see "Dovetail Layout" on p. 112).

4. Make the drawer stops from ¼-in.-thick wood and install two behind each drawer front to align it flush to the drawer case.

Finishing Up

1. Sand the case edging and the drawer fronts through 220 grit in preparation for finishing.

2. Apply a finish to the edging and drawer fronts. Burton wiped on four coats of a commercial oil and varnish blend, scrubbing between coats with 0000 steel wool.

PHOTO J: After chiseling out the bulk of the waste, use a wide flat chisel to pare down to the layout lines.

PHOTO K: To create each drawer front hand hole, drill two holes with a 2-in.-diameter bit; then saw between the lower quadrants with a jigsaw or bandsaw to complete the cutout.

Dovetail Cauls

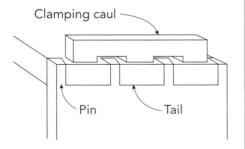

Clamping caul

Pin   Tail

If you need to clamp dovetail joints due to slightly loose fits or cupped boards, use notched cauls that span the pins.

MAN'S JEWELRY BOX

JUST AS WOMEN'S AND MEN'S JEWELRY differs, so do the boxes that contain it. A woman's jewelry box often incorporates many compartments and drawers to house a variety of rings, earrings, necklaces, pins, pendants, and bracelets. On the other hand, the collection of actual jewelry in a man's box might include only a couple of rings, a watch or two, cufflinks, and a few tie tacks. But that's not to say that's all you'll find in his box. You'll just as likely see a wallet or money clip, a pocket-knife, keys, a favorite pen, and perhaps a ticket stub from the 1966 World Series.

This cherry jewelry box was built by professional woodworker Allen Spooner, who designed it for a client as a birthday surprise for her husband. She wanted a simple but unique box that would sit nicely on top of a particular chest of drawers. For the box top, Spooner veneered a piece of hardwood plywood with book-matched cherry crotch veneer. To provide a nice contrast, as well as a touch of elegance, he used bird's-eye maple for the trim and edging. The box incorporates two inner sliding trays and a full mortise lock.

MAN'S JEWELRY BOX

This jewelry box is built mostly of solid stock. The top is ½"-thick veneered plywood edged with solid wood. The bottom is ¼"-thick plywood. The applied trim is sawn from solid stock, and two ledges inset in the box walls support sliding trays.

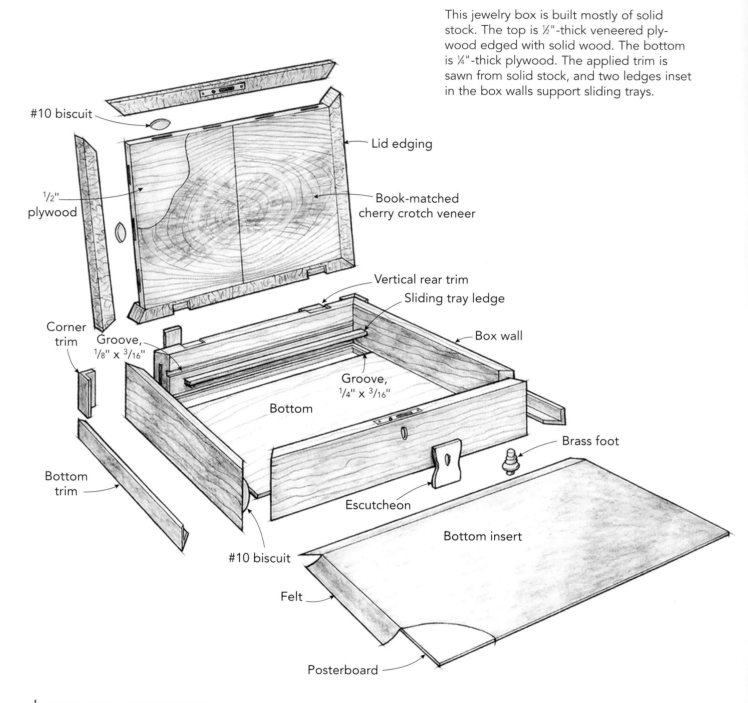

#10 biscuit

Lid edging

½" plywood

Book-matched cherry crotch veneer

Vertical rear trim

Sliding tray ledge

Box wall

Corner trim

Groove, ⅛" x ³/₁₆"

Groove, ¼" x ³/₁₆"

Bottom

Brass foot

Bottom trim

Escutcheon

Bottom insert

#10 biscuit

Felt

Posterboard

DESIGN OPTIONS

◆ A single piece of fancy veneer could be substituted for the book-matched crotch veneer.

◆ To personalize the box, a monogram can be inlaid into the veneer.

Top, Side, and Front Views

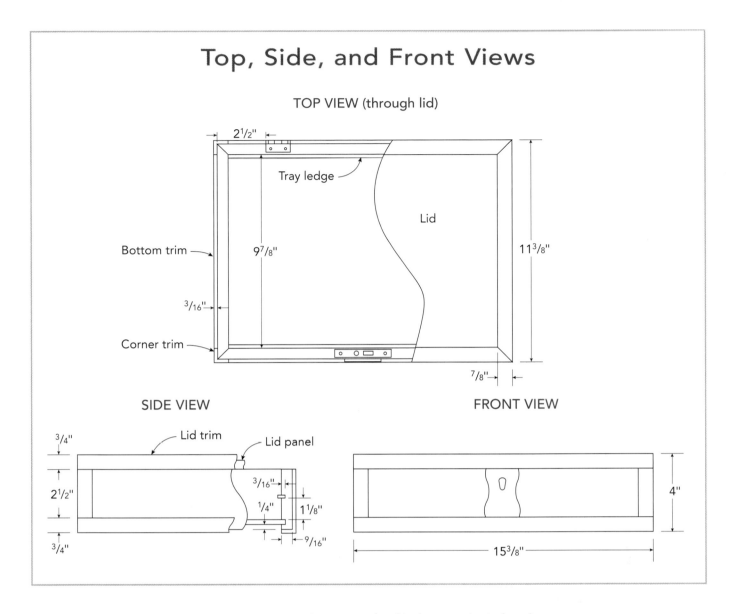

TOP VIEW (through lid)

2½"

Tray ledge

Lid

Bottom trim

9⅞"

11⅜"

3/16"

Corner trim

7/8"

SIDE VIEW

FRONT VIEW

3/4"

Lid trim

Lid panel

2½"

3/16"

¼"

1⅛"

4"

3/4"

9/16"

15⅜"

THIS ELEGANT LITTLE BOX shows how much can be done with simple joinery. A few grooves and miters, combined with biscuit joinery, are essentially all that's required here.

The box uses two different biscuit joinery setups. The box corners are first mitered and then biscuit joined with a 45-degree setup. The top also employs biscuits, but there to edge-join the trim section to the veneered panel.

Constructing the Box

Make the box body

1. Mill the stock for the box sides, front, and back to thickness and width. Leave the pieces a couple of inches oversize in length for right now.

2. Saw the grooves for the bottom panel and the tray ledges.

3. Cut the pieces to length and miter their ends using a good crosscut sawblade.

4. Cut the biscuit slots in the miters. Each joint gets one #10 biscuit. Alternatively, you could use splines.

5. Cut the bottom to fit snugly into its grooves. Spooner used a piece of cherry plywood for an attractive underview, but you could use any hardwood plywood.

6. Sand the bottom and the inside faces of the box walls; then dry-clamp the parts together to check for good joint fit.

CUT LIST FOR MAN'S JEWELRY BOX

2	Sides	9/16" x 3 1/16" x 11"	solid wood
2	Front/back	9/16" x 3 1/16" x 15"	solid wood
1	Bottom	1/4" x 10 1/4" x 14 1/4"	hardwood plywood
1	Top panel	1/2" x 9 5/8" x 13 5/8"	hardwood plywood
2	Top edgings	3/4" x 7/8" x 11 3/8"	solid wood
2	Top edgings	3/4" x 7/8" x 15 3/8"	solid wood
2	Bottom trims	3/4" x 3/4" x 11 3/8"	solid wood
2	Bottom trims	3/4" x 3/4" x 15 3/8"	solid wood
4	Corner trims	3/4" x 3/4" x 2 1/2"	solid wood
2	Rear vertical trims	3/16" x 1 1/4" x 2 1/2"	solid wood
2	Tray ledges	1/8" x 3/16" x 13 7/8"	solid wood
4	Tray sides	1/4" x 1 1/4" x 4 3/8"	solid wood
4	Tray sides	1/4" x 1 1/4" x 9 13/16"	solid wood
2	Tray bottoms	1/8" x 4 3/8" x 9 9/16"	hardwood plywood
1	Escutcheon	3/16" x 2" x 2 1/2"	solid wood
Other materials			
	Veneer	approx. 3' sq.	
2	Brass hinges	1 1/4" x 5/8"	*from* Woodcraft; item #13B17
1	Full-mortise lock	1 5/8" x 1 3/16"	*from* Woodcraft; item #13J61
	Felt	approx. 1' sq.	
4	Brass feet	3/8" high (exposed)	*from* Woodcraft; item #16B36

7. Glue up the sides and bottom, spot-gluing the bottom into its grooves to prevent rattling. Pull the miter joints together using a band clamp or miter clamping cauls (see "Miter Clamping Cauls" on p. 40). Make sure that the box sits flat and square under clamp pressure.
8. Sand the outsides of the box walls through 220 grit.

Veneer the top panel

The box top is a piece of 1/2-in.-thick plywood veneered on both sides with book-matched crotch cherry. Although you don't need to book-match both faces, they should both be veneered to ensure panel stability.

1. Cut the plywood panel for the top, leaving it slightly oversize for right now. Also cut a couple of panels of 3/4-in.-thick medium-density fiberboard (MDF) about 1 in. wider and longer than the plywood panel. You'll use these as clamping cauls when applying the veneer.
2. Prepare the veneers by book-matching each pair of halves so that the resulting sheets will be slightly larger than the plywood panel (see "Book-Matching Veneer").
3. Apply an even coat of white glue to one side of the plywood; then place the plywood onto the veneer. Coat the other side of the plywood and apply the remaining veneer. Press the veneer into the glue on both sides using a hard roller or straight-sided glass jar.
4. Sandwich the veneered panel between the two MDF cauls, with plastic wrap between to serve as a glue resist. Clamp the entire assembly tightly and let dry thoroughly (see **photo A** on p. 124).
5. Sand off the veneer tape, being careful not to sand through the thin veneer. Then saw the panel to size.

Trim the box

1. Mill enough long lengths of solid-wood stock to make up the top edging and box trim.
2. Saw the 9/16-in. by 9/16-in. rabbet in the trim stock for the box bottom and corners. For safety, use featherboards to hold the stock against the fence (see **photo B** on p. 124).
3. Fit the trim pieces that encircle the bottom edges of the box. Glue them in place using a band clamp and bar clamps.
4. Fit the vertical corner pieces tightly against the bottom trim and flush with the top edges of the box walls. Glue them in place using a band clamp.
5. Carefully miter the ends of the top edging pieces for a tight fit around the perimeter of the veneered panel.
6. Cut the biscuit slots for attaching the edging. When cutting the slots in the panel, slip a piece of veneer under the biscuit joiner

BOOK-MATCHING VENEER

Veneering a panel using two "mirrored" pieces of veneer yields a very attractive result, called "book-matching." Presliced, book-matched veneers can be purchased commercially or you can slice your own on the bandsaw (see "Resawing on the Bandsaw" on p. 26).

1. Begin by selecting and marking out the joint line on one of the pieces. Then cut to the line using a properly sharpened veneer saw and thick straightedge (see top photo at right).

2. Lay the sawn piece of veneer onto its twin, with the grain opposing. Then shift the two pieces in relation to each other until you've obtained a good mirror match (see middle photo at right). Mark the second joint line from the first; then saw it.

3. Join the two pieces with veneer tape on the show side of the veneer (see bottom photo at right). Pull the joint together with short pieces of tape, then tape the entire joint.

Veneer Sawing Tips

✦ Saw on a hardwood plywood platform, cutting cross-grain to the plywood.

✦ A piece of straight, square-edged, ¾-in.-thick MDF makes a great straightedge. Gluing sandpaper to the underside helps prevent slippage when cutting. To ensure a square-edged joint, lay the straightedge on the finished piece, not the offcut.

✦ Using a properly sharpened veneer saw, press it firmly against the edge of the straightedge to hold the saw vertical.

✦ Your initial saw strokes should be light, scoring cuts; subsequent cuts can be heavier. Make each pass using one full stroke, rocking the blade gradually in one direction through the arc of its toothed edge.

PHOTO A: Spooner glues the veneer to both faces of the top panel, covers the veneer faces with plastic wrap, and clamps the assembly between MDF cauls.

fence to offset the slots a bit. This ensures that the interior veneer won't project beyond the trim.

7. Glue the edging to the top panel with #0 biscuits.

Make the trays

1. Mill the tray ledge strips and glue them into their grooves.

2. Make the sliding trays. The corners are simple rabbet joints, and the bottoms are captured in grooves in the tray walls. Sand the inside faces of the parts before assembly, and the outsides afterward.

Installing the Hardware

Spooner used brass hinges that stop at 100 degrees open to prevent the lid from flopping backward. The full-mortise lock catches automatically when closed. (Don't lose the key or lock it in the box!)

Install the hinges

1. Lay out the hinge mortises in the box lid first. Align the rear of the hinge with the rear edge of the lid and trace around the hinge leaf with a sharp knife.

PHOTO B: When sawing the rabbets in the bottom and corner trim pieces, use a featherboard to prevent the stock from collapsing onto the sawblade.

Sliding Trays

The trays are built of solid wood, joined at the corners with rabbet joints. The ⅛"-thick bottoms are captured in grooves sawed into the walls.

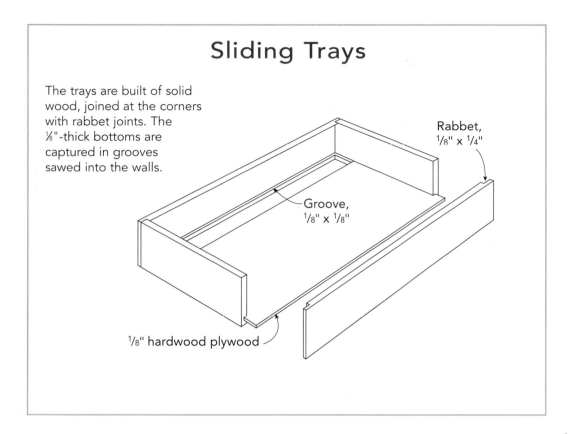

Rabbet, ⅛" x ¼"

Groove, ⅛" x ⅛"

⅛" hardwood plywood

2. Chisel each mortise to the depth of the hinge leaf. Or rout the mortises and square up their corners with a chisel afterward.

3. Install the hinges into their mortises with a single screw each. Place the lid on the box and run a knife along the ends of the hinge leaves and into the top edge of the rear box wall.

4. Lay out the hinge mortises on the box wall. To calculate the setback of the mortise from the outside of the rear wall, first find the distance between the hinge barrel and the inside edge of the leaf and then subtract the box lid overhang.

5. Chisel or rout the box wall mortises; then install the hinges into them with one screw each. Close the box lid and check its alignment to the box corners. Make any necessary adjustments to the hinge placement and then reinstall the hinges using new screw holes.

6. Chisel out a small notch at the top of each rear corner trim piece to provide clearance for the open lid (see **photo C** on p. 127).

Install the lock, escutcheon, and rear trim

1. Lay out and cut the mortise for the lock. (See "Installing a Full-Mortise Lock" on p. 126.)

2. Temporarily install the lock; then lay out the mortise for the catch. Using a square, extend lines from the edges of the lock bolt onto the face of the box. Close the lid and transfer the lines onto it to establish the length of the mortise. To determine the mortise setback, measure from the front of the box back to the bolt and add the thickness of the corner trim pieces.

3. Position the catch plate on the lid. Knife around its edges and then cut the shallow mortise that will set the plate flush into the box lid.

4. Make the escutcheon (see the pattern on p. 127). Mark out its keyhole slot and cut it out with a scrollsaw or fretsaw.

5. Glue the escutcheon to the box with the lock installed for backup support.

6. Make and fit the two pieces of vertical trim for the back. Glue them in place.

TIP

When sawing plywood on the table saw, always feed the pieces with the show side face up (for example, the outside face of case sides, the upper face of shelves). That way, any tearout will be on the hidden face.

INSTALLING A FULL-MORTISE LOCK

A full-mortise lock adds a classy touch to a piece of woodwork. The lock is strong and discrete, displaying only a keyhole, which you can augment with a metal or wood escutcheon. Different makes may employ different catch mechanisms, but the basic installation is the same for all full-mortise locks.

1. Lay out the keyhole location. Measure from the outermost edge of the lock's faceplate down to the center of its keyhole and transfer that measurement onto your workpiece, marking in from its edge.

2. Using a bit that matches the diameter of the lock's keyhole, drill the keyhole, stopping it short of the back of the workpiece. Then

drill overlapping holes below it to create an elongated opening for the key. Pare the sides of the opening flat (see left photo below).

3. Lay out the mortise for the lock body, carefully aligning the lock's keyhole with the one in the workpiece.

4. Drill or rout the mortise. Clamp scrap wood to the workpiece to provide support for the thin mortise walls (see right photo below). Clean up the faces and corners of the mortise with a chisel afterward.

5. Insert the lock and knife around the faceplate. Chisel out the shallow faceplate mortise until the faceplate sits down flush into it.

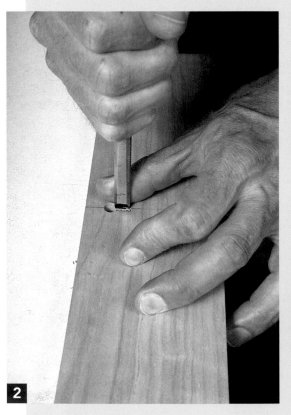

PHOTO C: Cut a small notch in the upper ends of the rear trim pieces to accommodate the swing of the lid. The rear vertical trim pieces fill in the hinge overhang.

Finishing Up

1. With the hardware still installed, sand the edges of the top flush to the box trim and escutcheon. Then finish-sand all of the trim through 220 grit.

2. Remove the hardware and finish the box and top. Spooner stained all of the pieces with Minwax cherry stain and then applied a coat of sealer and several coats of lacquer. An oil or wiping varnish finish would also be fine.

3. Make posterboard inserts for the box and tray bottoms. Wrap the top faces of the inserts with felt, pulling the excess tightly around underneath and gluing it to the bottom of the posterboard (see "Man's Jewelry Box" on p. 120).

4. Reinstall the hardware and attach the brass feet.

Escutcheon

Full size

MOBILE CLOSET

IT'S NOT UNUSUAL FOR AN APARTMENT or house to lack closet space. And it's often simply not feasible to construct a built-in closet, especially if you're renting. Well, here's an unusual solution, a closet that's both easy to make and extremely portable.

Furniture maker Denis Kissane designed this portable closet as an entry for a national design competition, where it won an award in the "contract furniture" division. Kissane intended it for use in hostels and hotels, but has found it to also be very popular for guest bedrooms. The open case makes the unit lightweight and allows clothes to air out.

Kissane used a commercially made chrome clothes bar, but you could use dowel rod instead.

Because it was designed for production, the closet is fairly easy to make. The tops, shelves, and divider are all the same width, and the tops and shelves are all the same length. Kissane built the case from cherry plywood, complimenting it with solid maple drawer fronts, posts, and rails. For aesthetic reasons, he made the case top, bottom, and divider 1 in. thick, gluing together ¾-in.-thick plywood and ¼-in.-thick plywood. But if you like, you can simply make those pieces from ¾-in.-thick plywood to save on time and materials.

MOBILE CLOSET

All the panels are edged with ¼"-thick solid wood and then joined together with #10 biscuits. The posts and rails are also joined to the case with biscuits. The drawers ride on center-mounted wooden slides.

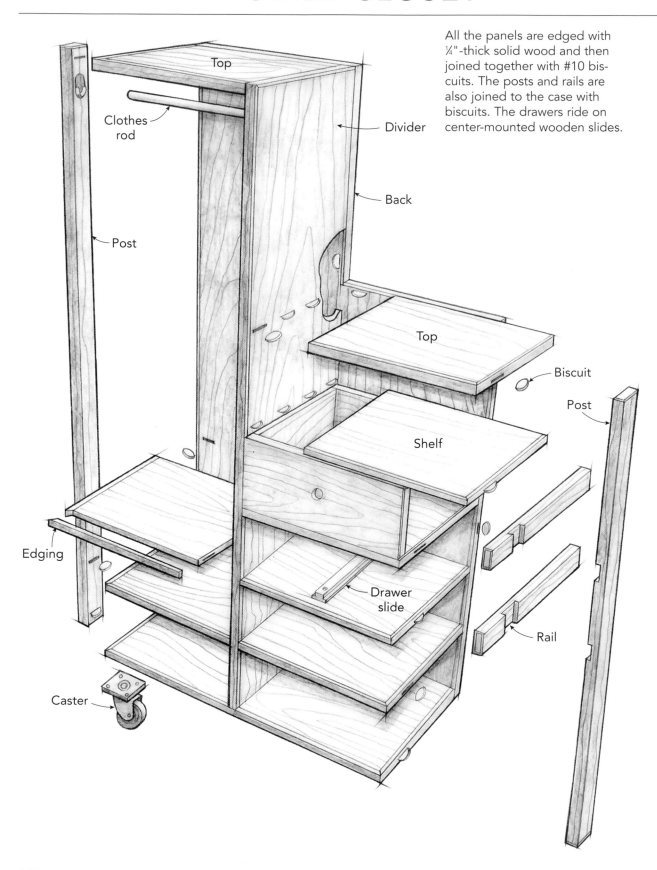

Top

Clothes rod

Divider

Back

Post

Top

Biscuit

Post

Shelf

Edging

Drawer slide

Rail

Caster

Side and Front Views

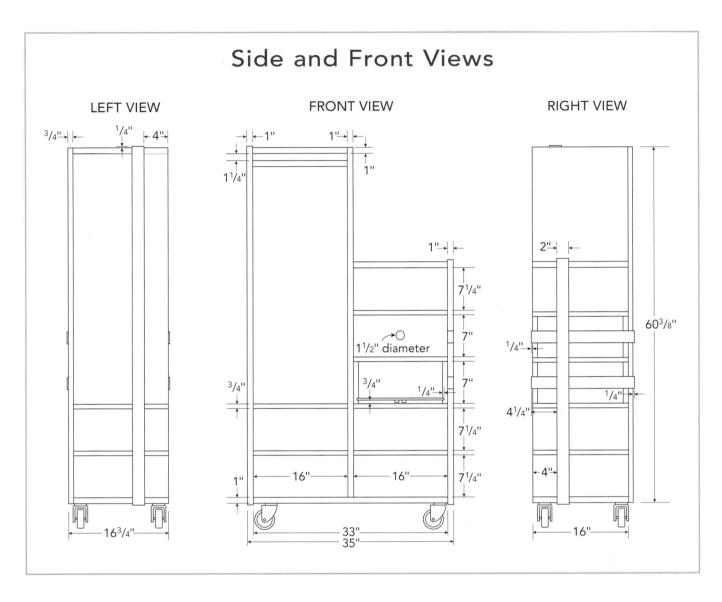

LEFT VIEW   FRONT VIEW   RIGHT VIEW

DESIGN OPTIONS

- Use ¾-in.-thick plywood for the divider, top, and bottom.

- Totally enclose the cabinet with sides and overlay doors.

- Install more drawers in the compartments and use commercial pulls, if desired.

- Install an overlay door over the clothes rod compartment.

BEGIN BY MAKING THE CASE and then the drawers. You'll saw all of the plywood pieces to size and then apply edging to them. After milling the posts and rails, you'll cut the joints and assemble the case. All that remains at that point is to make the drawers and apply a finish.

Building the Case

Make the pieces

1. Inspect your plywood sheets in preparation for laying out the parts. I shut off my overhead shop lights, draw the window blinds, and use a strong sidelight to inspect for scratches, dings, and imperfections (see **photos A** and **B** on p. 133).

CUT LIST FOR MOBILE CLOSET

Case

1	Divider	¾" x 15¾" x 59⅛" (59⅜")	hardwood plywood
1	Divider	¼" x 15¾" x 59⅛" (omit)	hardwood plywood
2	Tops	¾" x 15¾" x 15¾"	hardwood plywood
2	Tops	¼" x 15¾" x 15¾" (omit)	hardwood plywood
1	Bottom	¾" x 15¾" x 32½" (32¼")	hardwood plywood
1	Bottom	¼" x 15¾" x 32½" (omit)	hardwood plywood
6	Shelves	¾" x 15¾" x 15¾"	hardwood plywood
1	Back	¾" x 32½" (32¼") x 60⅛"	hardwood plywood
1	Post	1" x 2" x 60⅞"	solid wood
1	Post	1" x 2" x 41¼"	solid wood
2	Rails	1" x 2" x 17¼"	solid wood
	Edging	¼" x appropriate width and length	solid wood

Drawers

4	Front/backs	¾" x 6⅞" x 15⅞"	solid wood
4	Sides	¾" x 6⅞" x 14⁷⁄₁₆"	solid wood
2	Bottoms	¼" x 14¹⁵⁄₁₆" x 14⅞"	hardwood plywood

Other materials

2	Drawer slides (wood; center mount)		from Rockler; item # 24877
4	Casters (total-lock)	3"	from Rockler; item # 31870
1	Oval clothes rod (chrome)		from Woodworkers Hardware; item #KV0880 CHR96

If using ¾"-thick tops, dividers, and bottom, cut to dimensions in parentheses.

2. Lay out the parts for the tops, shelves, bottom, and divider. If the plywood has imperfections, try to hide them on the undersides of shelves or within the drawer compartments.

3. Cut the pieces. If you're going to make the tops, divider, and bottom 1 in. thick, as Kissane did, cut all those pieces slightly over-size in length and width. You'll trim them to final size afterward. If you're going to simply use ¾-in.-thick material for those parts, go ahead and cut them to final size now.

4. Glue together the ¼-in.-thick and ¾-in.-thick plywood to make the 1-in. thickness for the tops, divider, and bottom. As these are fairly large panels and you may not have the panel-pressing equipment, this may be a time to improvise. You can weigh down the panels with a sheet of ¾-in.-thick particleboard loaded down with cinderblocks or other heavy objects.

5. Saw the laminated panels to final size.

6. Lay out the back panel. When marking for the L-shaped cutout, remember to account for the ¼-in.-thick solid-wood edging all around the panel edges.

7. Saw the back panel. After cutting it to length and width, saw the L-shaped cutout. You can make the longer cut on the table saw, stopping short at the end and finishing the cut with a jigsaw. The shorter cut can be made by guiding a portable circular saw against a straightedge. Make the cut a bit wide; then rout to the cut line with a straight bit to smooth the edge.

8. Plane, joint, rip, and crosscut the rails and posts to size. At the same time, mill a couple extra short pieces of stock to use for test material when setting up the saw to cut the post-and-rail half-lap joint.

TIP

Although contact cement is a very convenient way of laminating panels, many woodworkers have found that the bond can be unreliable in the long run. If you don't want to risk future delamination, use white or yellow glue instead.

9. Make the edging, ripping the strips from a board that you've planed to ¹⁄₁₆ in. thicker than the edge to be covered. Also, crosscut the strips to about ¼ in. oversize in length. The edging will be trimmed flush to the plywood after attaching it.

Apply and trim the edging

There's quite a bit of mitered edging to apply to these pieces. If you work systematically and carefully, the work should go fairly quickly—and the result will be beautiful.

1. In preparation for the next steps, lay out the pieces for orientation, marking the rear edges of the pieces with triangles (see "Triangle Marking System" on p. 18).

2. Miter one end of each edging piece for the tops and shelves. Glue one of each pair to its plywood, carefully lining up the inside of the miter with the corner of the plywood. The ends opposite the miters should run a bit long, but you'll trim them later (see **photo C**).

3. After the glue cures, rout and plane the first piece of edging flush to the plywood (see **photo D** on p. 134). Then attach the remaining piece, also routing and planing it flush after the glue cures.

4. Fit the edging pieces to the case bottom. Carefully miter both ends of the front piece first, glue it in place, and trim it flush. Then fit and attach the side edging pieces, leaving them a bit long at the rear.

5. Fit and attach the edging to the divider and back. Try to fit the long pieces closely to length. You'll be paring the excess later, as it will be difficult to trim off on the table saw. Use cauls as necessary to distribute clamping pressure evenly on the edging.

6. Trim the square end of each edging piece flush to the plywood using a shim on the table saw (see **photo E** on p. 134). Because the divider and back can be awkward to feed on the table saw, flush up their ends using a very sharp chisel.

7. Finish-sand the faces of all the plywood panels now, because sanding into the cor-

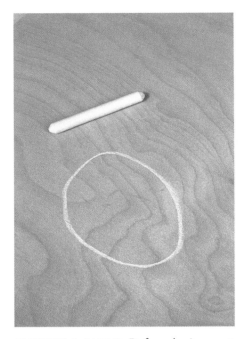

PHOTOS A AND B: Before laying out your plywood, inspect it for flaws using a strong, glancing sidelight in a darkened shop. The scar circled in chalk in the left photo is barely visible in normal light, but under a sidelight (right photo), it's immediately apparent.

PHOTO C: When fitting mitered edging pieces to length, rest the panels on thin shims and carefully align the inner edge of each miter to its panel corner. Test the fit by holding the adjacent pieces of mitered edging in place against the first miters.

ners will be difficult after assembly. Don't sand the edges yet. You'll do that after assembly.

Make the post-and-rail assembly

1. Lay out the half-lap joints that connect the rails to the right-hand post, as shown in the drawing on p. 130. The post is set back 4¼ in. from the front ends of the rails.

2. Mount a dado blade on your table saw and adjust its height to about ⁷⁄₁₆ in.

3. Using the extra pieces of stock you milled, fine-tune the height of the blade to cut exactly halfway through each piece. The easiest approach is to take a cut at each end of a piece and then fit them together for a look. Re-adjust the height of the blade a bit, take another pass on each piece, and check again. Repeat until the pieces are flush.

4. Glue and clamp the rails to the posts.

5. Using a sharp block plane, cut a small chamfer completely around the end of each post and rail.

PHOTO D: A laminate trimmer with a flush-trimming bit quickly routs the edging flush to the plywood panel. Afterward, smooth the joint with a block plane set for a very fine cut.

PHOTO E: To trim the ends of the edging, clamp a shim to your rip fence, aligning it with the outside edges of the sawteeth.

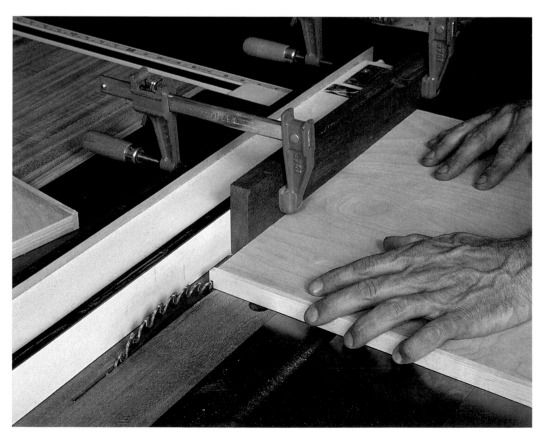

PHOTO F: After laying out the location of the top face of each shelf on the divider, clamp the shelf upside down with its edge aligned to the layout line. Mark the biscuit slot locations on the underside of the shelf.

Cut the biscuit joints

Now that all the parts are prepared, you're ready to cut the biscuit joints. If you don't have a biscuit joiner, you could dowel all of the parts together, working very carefully to align the dowel holes.

1. Lay out the shelf and right-hand top locations on the divider. Also lay out the divider location on the bottom. You need only gauge a short line where the top edge of each shelf meets the divider and where one side of the divider meets the bottom.

2. Lay out and cut the biscuit slots for the shelves and for the divider-to-bottom joint (see **photos F** and **G** and **photo H** on p. 136).

3. Lay out and cut the biscuit slots for joining the left-hand top to the divider. Right-angle joints like this involve registering the drop-down fence on the biscuit joiner against the end of the divider and the top edge of the shelf (see photo G on p. 105).

4. Lay out and cut the biscuit slots for joining the tops, bottom, shelves, and divider to the back.

5. Lay out and cut the biscuit slots for joining the posts and rails to the case. Note that the ends of the posts and rails all extend ¼ in. past the case edges.

PHOTO G: Set the biscuit joiner for a #10 slot, align the center index line on the bottom of the joiner with the biscuit location mark, and plunge into the divider.

PHOTO H: Register the base of the biscuit jointer on the divider, align the biscuit joiner center index line with the biscuit location mark, and plunge into the edge of the shelf. The parts should now align perfectly.

large enough to reach from the edge of the shelf to the post, you can use band clamps.

5. Glue and clamp the back in place. Use thick, long, crowned cauls to distribute clamp pressure across the joints (see "Clamping Cauls" on p. 19).

6. Glue and clamp the post-and-rail assembly to the right-hand side of the case, again spanning the post with cauls if you don't have deep-throat clamps. Alternatively, you could attach the assembly with screws though counterbored holes, which you could plug later.

7. After the glue cures, plane or scrape all adjacent joints flush to each other.

Building the Drawers

The drawers are easy to make. They are simply boxes biscuited together at the corners. The bottoms sit in grooves routed in the front, sides, and back. The drawers ride on center-mounted wooden drawer slides.

Make the drawers

1. Cut the fronts, backs, and sides to size.

2. Rout the ¼-in. by ¼-in. grooves in all of the pieces to accept the drawer bottoms. The grooves sit ¾ in. up from the bottom edge of the pieces. The grooves in the front and back stop ½ in. from the ends.

3. Lay out and cut the slots at the corners for the #10 biscuits. Cut the lowest slots as close as possible to the drawer bottom groove without intruding into it.

4. On the drill press, bore the 1½-in.-diameter finger hole through the center of each drawer front.

5. Saw the drawer bottoms to size.

6. Dry-assemble the drawers to check the joint fit.

7. Glue and clamp the drawers. Make sure they are sitting on a flat surface and that they're square while under clamp pressure. Spot glue the bottoms into their grooves. Let the glue cure thoroughly.

Fit the drawers

Kissane used commercially available wooden slides, but you could make your own.

Assemble the case

Gluing up the case needs to be done in stages. Because of the lack of case sides to help hold the pieces in place, assembly can be a bit awkward. Get a helper if you can and definitely rehearse every clamp-up procedure before getting out the glue bottle. After gluing each joint, immediately clean up excess glue with a clean rag and clean water.

1. Assemble the right-hand top and right-hand shelves to the divider. Use thick hardwood cauls to span the divider and pull the joint together tightly. Make sure everything is square under clamp pressure. Temporarily screwing a brace to the opposite ends of the shelves will help stabilize them. Attach the screws at the post location.

2. Glue and clamp the left-hand top and shelves to the divider.

3. Glue the divider to the bottom. You can use screws instead of clamps to pull this joint home.

4. Glue and clamp the left-hand post in place. If you don't have a deep-throat clamp

1. Fit the drawer half of the slide to the drawer, notching out the bottom edges of the drawer front and back and then gluing the slide in place (see "Drawer Slides"). Make certain that the slide is mounted perpendicular to the drawer front.

2. Cut the case half of each slide to length. The front end of the slide should stop ¾ in. short of the front edge of the shelf.

3. Center the case half of each slide across the width of its shelf and tack it in place with a small finish nail at each end. Insert the drawer and check to make sure it's centered. If necessary, tap the case half of the slide to better position it. When the drawer is centered, attach the slide using flat-head screws, countersinking them into the slide.

4. Check the gap all around the drawer to make sure it's consistent. If necessary, plane or sand the edges for a neat ¹⁄₁₆-in. reveal all around the front. To create the reveal at the bottom of the drawer front, plane it to create a bevel that rises slightly upward from the rear edge of the front.

5. Sand the drawers through 220 grit. Take care not to round over the exposed edges and corners too much. You want a crisp, but friendly look here.

Finishing Up

1. Touch-up sand the panel faces where the grain was raised by the glue cleanup. Using 220-grit sandpaper, gently round over all edges and corners without over-sanding them.

2. Apply a finish. Kissane sprayed the closet with several coats of lacquer, but you could use any finish you like. Although the unit isn't likely to suffer much water or alcohol damage, the finish should be tough enough to resist some abrasion.

3. Attach the casters. Kissane used heavy-duty, locking swivel casters, which ensure safety and allow great maneuverability.

4. Install the clothes rod brackets and cut the rod to size. Kissane used a commercial, oval-shaped, chrome rod, but you could use a wooden rod from a home-supply store.

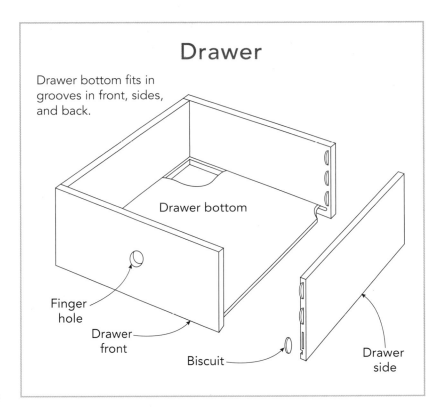

Drawer

Drawer bottom fits in grooves in front, sides, and back.

Drawer bottom

Finger hole

Drawer front

Biscuit

Drawer side

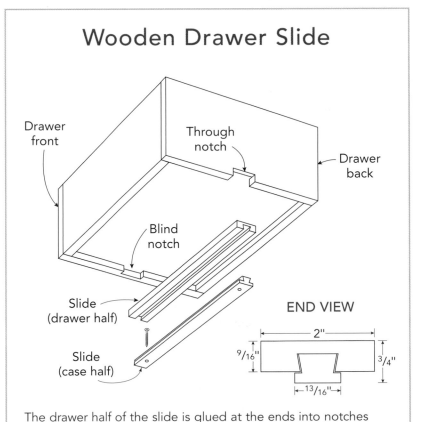

Wooden Drawer Slide

Drawer front

Through notch

Drawer back

Blind notch

Slide (drawer half)

Slide (case half)

END VIEW

2"

⁹⁄₁₆"

³⁄₄"

¹³⁄₁₆"

The drawer half of the slide is glued at the ends into notches cut into the drawer front and back. The case half is screwed to the shelf with countersunk flat-head screws.

STORAGE BENCH

SOME OF HE BEST STORAGE SOLUTIONS are multipurpose. This lovely little cherry bench is a good example. Professional furniture maker Peter Turner designed and built this for clients as a replacement for an antique bench they kept at the foot of their bed to hold magazines. Turner was invited to come up with a new design to complement the clients' new cherry bed. The splayed, slatted arms—reminiscent of a sleigh bed headboard—are complemented by simple but refined turned feet. Turner describes his creation as "Empire meets Shaker."

This project involves template routing and a bit of turning. There's no wood bending involved; all of the curved parts are sawn from solid stock. The basic framework is constructed with standard mortise-and-tenon joinery. The only really tricky part is fitting the tops of the slats into the mortises, which involves some careful handwork.

Although this bench was designed for a bedroom, it would be equally at home in a foyer, living room, or dining room. The drawers can hold anything from scarves and gloves to reading material to bed or table linens.

STORAGE BENCH

Mortise-and-tenon joinery connects the framework. The solid-wood platform is glued to the front rail and floats free in the side and rear rails grooves. The curved legs and slats are bandsawn and template routed from solid stock. The top ends of the slats fit into mortises in the arm rails.

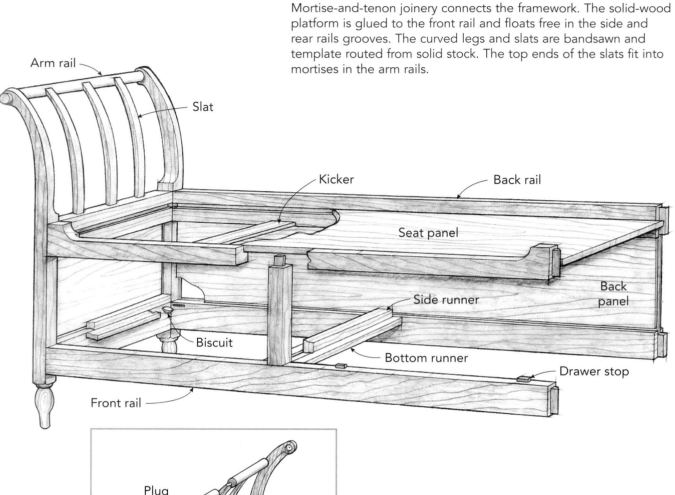

Arm rail

Slat

Kicker

Back rail

Seat panel

Back panel

Side runner

Biscuit

Bottom runner

Drawer stop

Front rail

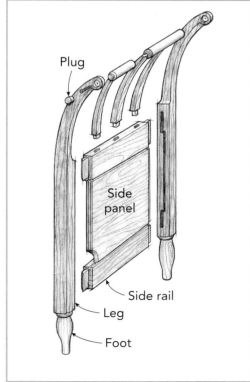

Plug

Side panel

Side rail

Leg

Foot

DESIGN OPTIONS

✦ The length of the bench can be modified to suit a particular space.

✦ Make the bench from wood that matches existing furniture.

✦ Fit a cushion to the bench.

Top, Front, and Side Views

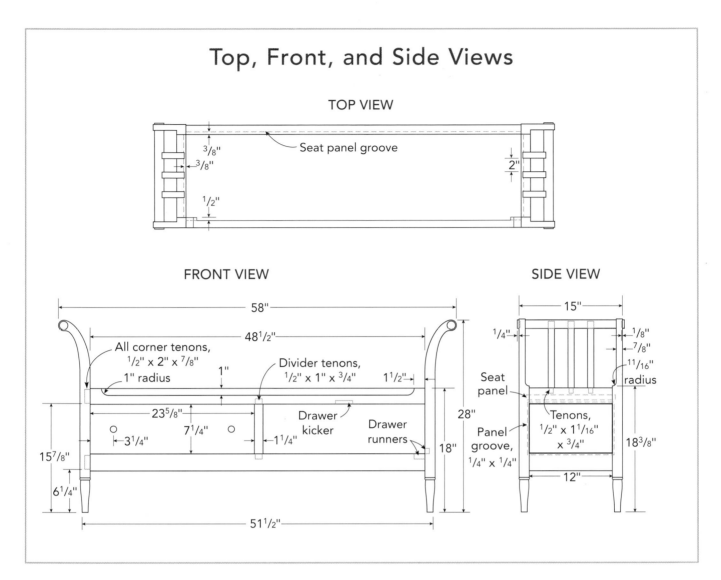

TOP VIEW

Seat panel groove

$3/8$"
$3/8$"
$1/2$"
2"

FRONT VIEW

58"

$48^{1}/2$"

All corner tenons,
$1/2$" x 2" x $7/8$"

1" radius

1"

Divider tenons,
$1/2$" x 1" x $3/4$"

$1^1/2$"

$23^5/8$"

Drawer
kicker

$7^1/4$"

$1^1/4$"

Drawer
runners

$3^1/4$"

$15^7/8$"

$6^1/4$"

28"

18"

$51^1/2$"

SIDE VIEW

15"

$1/4$"

$1/8$"

$7/8$"

$11/16$"
radius

Seat
panel

Tenons,
$1/2$" x $1^{11}/16$"
x $3/4$"

Panel
groove,
$1/4$" x $1/4$"

$18^3/8$"

12"

THIS LITTLE BENCH is a fairly challenging project because of the curved parts. But if you work carefully and in the proper sequence, it all comes together great. You'll make the legs first, then the rails; next, you'll fit the slats and panels. After assembling all the parts, you'll make the drawers and fit them into their openings.

Making the Legs

Shaping the legs involves sawing, template routing, and turning. After the legs are shaped, the joints are cut with a router.

Initial shaping of the profile

1. Make a full-size leg pattern on stiff paper. Include the layout for the rails and slats. Use

Corner Joinery

TOP VIEW

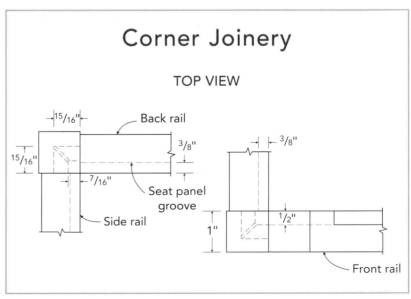

$15/16$"

Back rail

$3/8$"

$15/16$"

$7/16$"

Seat panel
groove

Side rail

$3/8$"

1"

$1/2$"

Front rail

CUT LIST FOR STORAGE BENCH

Bench			
4	Legs	1½" x 1½" x 28"	solid wood
1	Top front rail	1½" x 2¼" x 50¼"	solid wood
1	Top back rail	1⅜" x 2¼" x 50¼"	solid wood
1	Bottom front rail	1½" x 2½" x 50¼"	solid wood
1	Bottom back rail	1⅜" x 2½" x 50¼"	solid wood
2	Top side rails	1⅜" x 2¼" x 13¾"	solid wood
2	Bottom side rails	1⅜" x 2½" x 13¾"	solid wood
1	Drawer divider	1¼" x 1½" x 8¾"	solid wood
2	Bottom drawer runners	¾" x 1½" x 12"	solid wood
1	Bottom drawer runner	¾" x 4" x 12"	solid wood
2	Side drawer runners	¾" x ¾" x 12"	solid wood
1	Side drawer runner	⅞" x 1¼" x 12"	solid wood
2	Drawer kickers	½" x 2½" x 12"	solid wood
6	Slat blanks	⅞" x 3¼" x 11"	solid wood
2	Arm rails	1¼" diameter x 13½"	solid wood
1	Seat panel	¾" x 12⅞" x 49¼"	solid wood
2	Side panels	¾" x 7¾" x 12½"	solid wood
1	Back panel	¾" x 7¾" x 49"	solid wood
Drawers			
4	Drawer sides	9/16" x 7¼" x 13"	solid wood
4	Drawer front/ backs	9/16" x 7¼" x 23 9/16"	solid wood
2	Drawer bottoms	⅜" x 12⅜" x 22 15/16"	hardwood plywood
2	Drawer fronts	⅞" x 7¼" x 23 9/16"	solid wood
2	Pulls	15/16" diameter x 1⅝"	solid wood

Dimensions for all pieces with tenons include tenon length.

the paper pattern to make a leg profile pattern from ¼-in.-thick hardboard or plywood (see "Leg Pattern"). (You'll use the paper pattern again later to make a wood pattern for the slats.) To make the wood leg pattern, cut the straight sections on the table saw and the curved sections with a jigsaw or bandsaw; then fair the curves smooth with files and sandpaper. Using a 1/16-in.-diameter bit, drill through the center of the circular area at the top.

2. Mill stock for the legs. To maximize wood, Turner milled a 1½-in.-thick by 10-in.-wide by 10-ft.-long board, which yielded the legs and the rails (see "Leg and Rail Layout").

3. Joint both edges of the boards straight and square.

4. Using the leg pattern, lay out the legs with their straight inside edges against the jointed edges of the stock.

5. On the bandsaw, cut the concave edge of the leg to shape, staying 1/16 in. outside the cut line. Don't cut the convex edge yet.

6. On the table saw, cut the outer, straight section of the leg (see **photo A**). Alternatively, you could bandsaw the section oversize and then trim it with a router guided against a straightedge.

PHOTO A: Set up a featherboard to press the leg to the rip fence. Use a block to stop the cut after 18½ in.

Leg Pattern

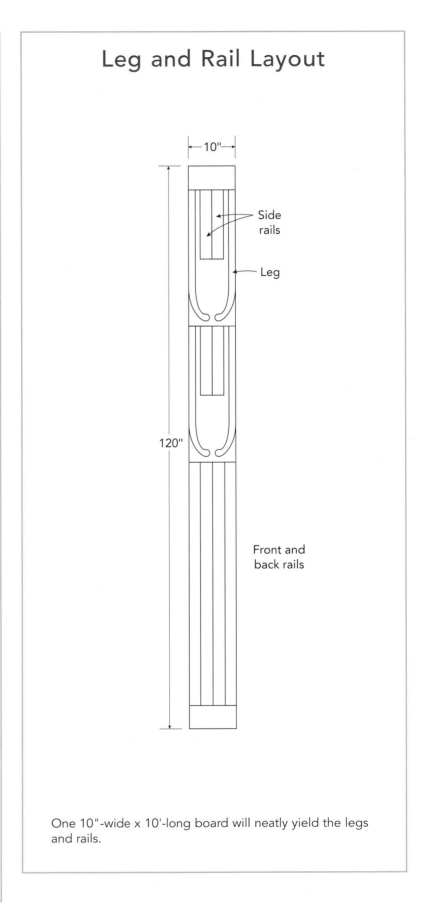

4³/₄"

3/8"

1¹/₂"

Slat

28"

3/4"

Panel

1/4"

Leg and Rail Layout

10"

Side rails

Leg

120"

Front and back rails

One 10"-wide x 10'-long board will neatly yield the legs and rails.

PHOTO B: After turning the foot area to a cylinder with a gouge and cutting a notch 5 in. up from the bottom of the leg, lay the skew chisel over and complete the cylinder.

PHOTO C: Use a very sharp skew chisel to cut the transition between square and cylindrical.

Turn the feet

Because you haven't yet sawn the convex section of the leg, that edge of your blank is straight the full length for mounting between the lathe centers. Turn the foot to the shape shown in "Foot Pattern" on p. 146. Run your lathe at the slowest speed possible because of the imbalanced work-piece. *Caution:* Stay well clear of the swinging splayed end as you turn the foot.

1. Turn the bottom 4¾ in. to a cylindrical shape using a gouge.

2. Using a skew chisel on edge, make a V-cut 5-in. up from the bottom.

3. Lay the skew over and complete the cylindrical section up to the V-cut (see **photo B**).

4. Cut the transition from square to cylindrical using a very sharp skew chisel to prevent tearout (see **photo C**).

5. Use the skew chisel to shape the upper part of the foot to create the ring (see **photo D**).

6. Shape the rest of the profile using a gouge (see **photo E**).

PHOTO D: Use a skew to shape the top of the curve, creating the ring above.

PHOTO E: Shape the rest of the foot profile with a gouge, cleaning up with a skew afterward.

Foot Pattern

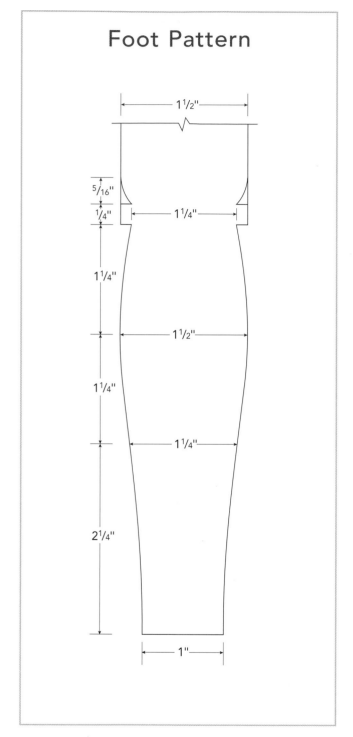

1 1/2"

5/16"

1/4"

1 1/4"

1 1/4"

1 1/2"

1 1/4"

1 1/4"

2 1/4"

1"

Router Template Jig
for the Legs

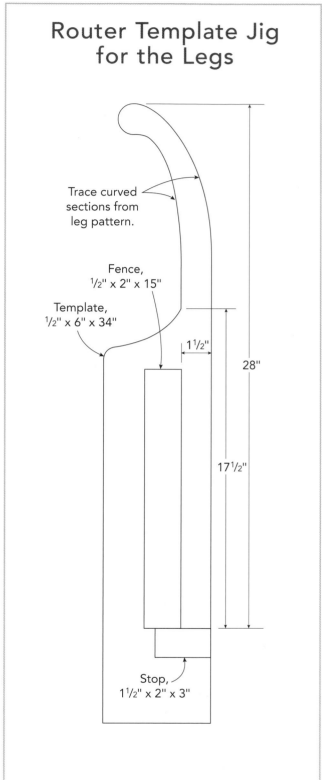

Trace curved
sections from
leg pattern.

Fence,
1/2" x 2" x 15"

Template,
1/2" x 6" x 34"

1 1/2"

28"

17 1/2"

Stop,
1 1/2" x 2" x 3"

PHOTO F: With the top of the leg held with double-sided tape and the body clamped to the template jig fence, rout the curved section using a flush-trimming bit. A support block taped to the router base keeps the router level.

PHOTO G: After drilling the curve in the inner face of the leg, use a bandsaw fence to guide the straight cut at the top of the leg.

Compete the leg profile

1. Bandsaw the convex curve, again staying about ⅟₁₆ in. outside of the cut line.

2. Using the layout pattern, make a template jig for routing the curved section of the leg (see "Router Template Jig for the Legs").

3. Fix each leg in turn to the template jig and rout the final profile using a flush-trimming bit (see **photo F**).

4. Mark out the ⅞-in.-thick section at the top of the leg.

5. Chuck a 1⅜-in.-diameter flat-bottom bit in your drill press, clamp a leg to the drill press fence, and drill for the transition between the top and bottom sections of each leg (see "Side View" on p. 141).

6. Bandsaw the top section of the leg to width (see **photo G**). To minimize cleanup, use a bandsaw fence set to accommodate drift (see "Resawing on the Bandsaw" on p. 26).

7. Clean up the bandsaw marks with a plane, scraper, and sandpaper.

PHOTO H: Rout the side and back panel grooves registering the router edge guide against the inner faces of the legs and rails.

Cut the leg mortises

1. Lay the leg pattern onto each leg and drill completely through the leg at the top to mark the center of the round rail. Use the drill press for accuracy.

2. Using a 1-in.-diameter flat-bottom bit, drill a ⅛-in.-deep hole on both sides of the leg at the top so the round rail and outer plugs can be added later, as shown in drawing on p. 140.

3. Lay out the mortises for the rails. Note that the mortises for the side and back rails are inset ¹⁄₁₆ in. more than the mortises for the front rail.

4. Rout the mortises ¹⁵⁄₁₆ in. deep using an edge guide on the router, registered against the inside face of each piece.

Make the rails

1. Plane, joint, rip, and crosscut the rails and drawer divider to size.

2. Lay out and rout the mortises for the drawer divider in the front rails.

3. Saw the rail and drawer divider tenons. Aim for a snug fit in the mortises. Afterward, round their edges with a file and chisel

to approximately match the radius on the ends of each mortise. Then cut the ends of the rail tenons at 45 degrees.

4. Dry-clamp the rails into their mortises to check the fit. If necessary, plane the inside face of each rail flush to the legs.

5. Rout the ¼-in. by ¼-in. panel grooves in the edges of the rails (see "Leg Pattern" on p. 143). Use a router edge guide, registering it on the inside face of each rail. Then, using the same edge guide setup, rout the mating panel grooves in the legs, again registering the edge guide against the inside faces (see **photo H**). Don't groove the legs at the drawer openings.

6. Cut the ¾-in.-wide by ⅜-in.-deep seat panel grooves 1 in. down from the top edge of the side and back rails. Make the groove ½ in. deep in the top front rail, as shown in "Corner Joinery" on p. 141. Use a dado head on the table saw.

7. Lay out the wide, U-shaped cutout on the top front rail. Then drill the curves using a 2-in.-diameter drill bit on the drill press.

8. Bandsaw the straight section of the cutout, staying about ¹⁄₁₆ in. outside the cut line. You'll rout to the cut line after assembling the bench.

9. Lay out the ½-in.-wide by 11⁄16-in.-long mortises in the top edge of the side rails to accept the slats as shown in the "Front and Side Views" drawing on p. 141.

10. Rout the mortises 13⁄16 in. deep. Because the tenon shoulders will only be ⅛ in. wide, take care to stay inside the layout lines. I clamped stop blocks to the rail to restrict router travel.

Constructing Drawer Runners and Kickers

Make the parts

1. Make the drawer runners and kickers, leaving them slightly oversize in length for right now.

2. Saw or rout the ⅛-in. by 1¼-in. groove in the center bottom runner to accept the center side runner.

Building the Slat and Arm Rails

Now you're ready to tackle the slats and arm rails. Making the parts is fairly easy, but fitting them can be a bit fussy.

Make the slats

1. Begin by making a full-size pattern of a slat from ¼-in.-thick hardboard or plywood (see "Leg Pattern" on p. 143). Use the full-size paper leg pattern that you made earlier and transfer the slat section to the wood with the help of carbon paper.

2. Use the pattern to make two template jigs: one for the convex curve and one for the concave curve (see "Router Template Jigs for the Slats").

3. Make the blanks for the slats. Mill a couple extras in case of mistakes.

4. Cut off one corner of each slat ½ in. from the bottom at a 20-degree angle so the piece will rest against both fences on jig 1.

5. Place the blank in template jig 1, trace the curve onto the blank, and then bandsaw about 1⁄16 in. outside the cut line.

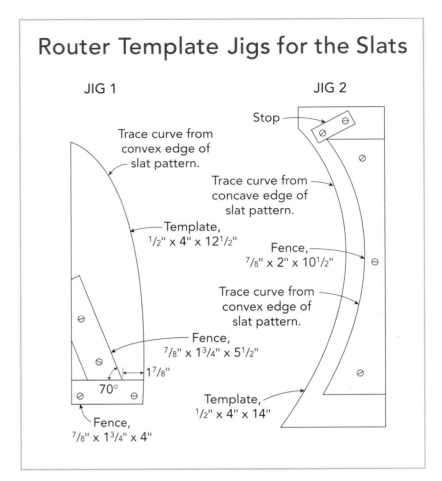

Router Template Jigs for the Slats

JIG 1

JIG 2

Stop

Trace curve from convex edge of slat pattern.

Trace curve from concave edge of slat pattern.

Template, ½" x 4" x 12½"

Fence, ⅞" x 2" x 10½"

Trace curve from convex edge of slat pattern.

Fence, ⅞" x 1¾" x 5½"

1⅞"

70°

Template, ½" x 4" x 14"

Fence, ⅞" x 1¾" x 4"

PHOTO I: After trimming off the bottom corner of the slat blank and bandsawing away most of the waste on the convex edge, the blank is ready for mounting on template jig 1.

6. Mount the blank in the template jig using double-sided tape or hot-melt glue (see **photo I** on p. 141).

7. Turn the template jig upside down and rout the convex curve on the router table using a flush-trimming bit (see **photo J**).

8. After removing the workpiece from the template jig, align your slat pattern with the bottom and curved edge of the blank. Then trace the top and concave edge of the pattern (see **photo K**).

9. Bandsaw just outside the layout lines as before.

10. Mount the slat into template jig 2, butting the top end against the jig's stop (see **photo L**). Then rout the concave curve in the same manner as you did the convex curve.

Make the slat tenons

1. Gauge a fine line fully around each slat ¾ in. up from the bottom to mark the tenon shoulders. Then mark the width of the tenon on one face.

2. Using a crosscut sled set up with a tall stop block, saw the tenon cheeks, keeping just shy of the shoulder line (see **photo M**).

PHOTO J: Turn the template jig upside down for template routing the convex curve. Feed the workpiece right to left against the bit.

PHOTO K: After template routing the convex edge, line up the plywood slat pattern with the bottom of the blank and trace the concave edge and top onto the blank for bandsawing.

PHOTO L: After bandsawing just outside of the pencil line, the slat is ready to be mounted in template jig 2 for routing the concave edge.

3. Pare to the shoulder lines using a very sharp chisel. Next, round the tenon edges with a file and chisel to match the ends of the mortise.

Turn the arm rails and end plugs

1. Saw the stock for the arms rails, and cut it to length. Make at least one extra rail in case of mistakes. Mortising the rails is one of the trickiest parts of making this bench.
2. Turn each arm rail blank to a 1¼-in.-diameter cylinder (see "Turning a Cylinder" on p. 152).
3. Turn a ⅛-in.-long by 1-in.-diameter tenon on each end of the rail using a parting tool (see **photo N** on p. 152). Check for a

PHOTO M: Support the slat against a stop block clamped to a crosscut sled to cut the tenon cheeks. Afterward, pare to the tenon shoulders with a sharp chisel.

TIP

When mounting a workpiece to a template or jig with double-sided tape or hot-melt glue, first apply wide, thick cellophane tape to the pieces to prevent damage when separating them later. To ensure that the double-sided tape holds well, tightly clamp the workpiece to the jig for a few moments.

PHOTO N: Use a parting tool to turn the tenon on each end of the arm rail.

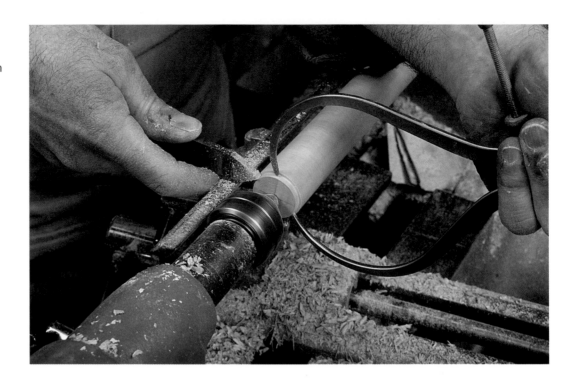

TURNING A CYLINDER

Turning a simple cylinder can be more difficult than shaping a fancy spindle because irregularities in a straight line tend to look obvious. Here's how to turn a straight-sided cylinder that's consistent in diameter.

1. Turn the blank roughly cylindrical using a gouge.

2. Set a caliper a bit wider than your desired diameter; then turn a series of grooves to the caliper opening (see top photo at right).

3. Using a gouge, cut the entire workpiece to the depth of the grooves.

4. Set a block plane for a fairly heavy cut. Holding it diagonally, move it across the spinning piece to remove gouge ridges and straighten the profile (see bottom photo at right).

snug fit in the round mortises that you drilled at the top of the legs.

4. Mark out the mortise spacing. Extend the lines fully around the rail while it's still on the lathe.

5. Turn a couple of short lengths of 1¼-in.-diameter stock with a ⅛-in.-long by 1-in.-diameter tenon on each end. Then slice ⅜-in. off the end of each piece to make the tenoned plugs that project ¼ in. from the tops of the legs.

Rout the arm-rail mortises

The mortises in the arm rails begin as short, routed slots that you then square and enlarge with chisels to accept the tops of the slats.

1. Chuck a ⁵⁄₁₆-in.-diameter straight bit in your table router and adjust it so it projects ⅝ in. above the table. Position the fence ¼ in. away from the perimeter of the bit.

2. Make two guide blocks for holding the rail in position for routing (see "Arm Rail Guide Blocks"). Attach the blocks to the rail with a couple of dabs of hot-melt glue on each end. Make sure the blocks are glued parallel to each other.

3. Draw two vertical lines on the fence that represent the cutting diameter of the bit. These will help you set up your stop blocks.

4. Place the rail-guide block assembly against the router table fence and clamp stop blocks to the fence to limit the assembly travel for routing the first mortise.

5. To rout a mortise, begin by holding the rail horizontally, pressing it against the fence and the right-hand stop. Lower the rail about ⅛ in. onto the spinning bit; then move it to the left until it contacts the left-hand stop. Make repeated cuts in the same manner until the blocks contact the router table (see **photo O**).

Chisel the mortises

Shaping the mortises to accept the top of the slats is the fussiest part of making this bench. But work carefully and methodically, and you'll do all right.

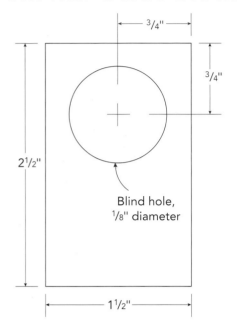

Arm Rail Guide Blocks

Two of these blocks position the arm rail for routing the slat mortises. Make the blocks from ¾"-thick stock. Dimension and drill them accurately.

PHOTO O: To mortise the arm rail, hold it by the guide blocks, lowering it in successive shallow passes onto the spinning bit. Move from right to left between the stops.

PHOTO P: Cut away only the corners on the thin-walled edge; then enlarge the mortise bit by bit on the opposing edge until it accepts the slat.

Building the Panels

The panels for the sides, back, and seat are all made of solid wood and fit unglued into their grooves to allow for seasonal wood movement.

Make the panels

1. Mill the stock for the panels, and edge-join the boards if necessary to make up the width of the panels. If edge-joining, take care to compose the grain nicely (see "Composing Grain for Panels" on p. 99).

2. Surface the panels; then cut them for an appropriate fit in their grooves (see "Fitting Solid-Wood Panels").

3. Notch the corners of the seat panel to fit tightly between the side assemblies and against both faces of the front legs. The panel will be glued to the front rail, so cut the face of each rear notch so it will allow for movement toward and away from the back legs.

4. Rabbet both faces of the back and side panels to create the ¼-in.-thick by ⁵⁄₁₆-in.-wide tongues that ride in the rail grooves. The outside face of each panel should be flush with the adjacent legs.

Assembling the Bench

Now it's time to put together all the parts you've made. You'll glue up the side assemblies first and then the front framework. Finally, you'll attach the side assemblies to the front and back rails.

Join the parts

1. Prepare for assembly by sanding all of the parts through 220 grit. Be careful not to round over ends and edges that meet flush, such as the junction of the front rails and legs. Also go easy at the tops of the slats where they insert in the mortises.

2. Apply at least one coat of finish to all of the panels. Don't get finish on the front edge of the seat panel, where it will be glued to the front rail.

3. Dry-fit the side assemblies to rehearse your clamping procedure. First place the side panel between the rails and insert the slat

1. Begin by squaring up the mortises, keeping the flat side of the chisel in the same plane as the mortise wall it's cutting (see **photo P**). Use very sharp chisels and be careful not to break out the thin section near what will be the top of the installed rail.

2. Widen the first mortise bit by bit until it accepts the slat. Pare only toward what will be the underside of the rail; don't cut away any more of the thin area toward the "top." Keep testing the fit until the top of the tenon slides snugly in place. You can also sand or pare the slats a bit to fit the mortises.

3. Pare the other mortises in the same manner. Occasionally reinsert the first slat and use it as a visual guide to keep the other slats parallel as you cut their mortises.

FITTING SOLID-WOOD PANELS

When fitting solid-wood panels into frames of any sort, allow for seasonal expansion and contraction across the grain. How much allowance depends the season of year the piece is built and the type of climate it will live in. Wood moves predominantly across the grain; movement along the grain is negligible. This means that you can fit the end-grain edges of a panel tightly between the frame grooves, but you need to build in space between the long-grain edges and their grooves.

During hot, humid weather, fit a panel fairly tightly. During the cold, dry season, allow for expansion. For stable woods like teak and mahogany, allow up to ⅛-in. movement per foot of width. For most domestic North American woods like cherry, oak, and walnut, figure somewhere between ⅛ in. and ¼ in. per foot of width. When dealing with a wide area, avoid using a single, wide panel, which might shrink out of

its grooves or blow a frame apart. Instead use several smaller panels, separating them with stiles or rails.

Prefinish solid-wood panels before installing them. Otherwise, shrinkage may expose a perimeter of raw wood later. To keep a panel centered in its frame, you can pin it at the center from behind with a small dowel or a bamboo skewer from the grocery store. Alternatively, you can apply small pieces of foam weather-stripping into the grooves, which will also prevent panel rattle.

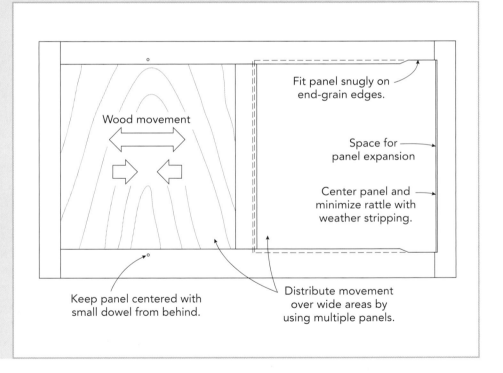

Wood movement

Fit panel snugly on end-grain edges.

Space for panel expansion

Center panel and minimize rattle with weather stripping.

Keep panel centered with small dowel from behind.

Distribute movement over wide areas by using multiple panels.

tenons into their mortises. Attach the legs; then splay them apart at the top to insert the arm rail (see **photo Q** on p. 156).

4. Drill a clearance hole through the top of each leg for driving a #6 by 2-in. screw into the arm rail.

5. Glue up both side assemblies. Use glue sparingly at the top of the slats and don't

glue the panels into their grooves. Glue and screw the legs to the arm rails.

6. Glue the front rails to the drawer divider, making sure that the assembly is flat and square under clamp pressure.

7. Dry-clamp the front and back rails to the side assemblies and trim the drawer runners and kickers for a snug fit between the front

PHOTO Q: Place the prefinished panel between the rails, insert the slats, and attach the legs. Then spread the legs apart at the top to attach the arm rail.

and back rails. Then cut the biscuit slots in the runners, kickers, and rails, as shown in the drawing on p. 140.

8. Next, glue the front edge of the seat panel to the front rail at the same time that you glue the runners and kickers in place. (You might want a helper for this step. Definitely rehearse your assembly procedures before spreading glue on anything.) Make sure the center runner is square to the front rails. Attach the side assemblies unglued to hold everything in place.

9. Glue the rails to one side assembly; then slip the back panel unglued into its grooves before gluing on the other side assembly. Make sure that the drawer openings are square when everything is clamped up.

10. Install a bottom-bearing flush-trimming bit in the router. Run the bearing along the

---

TIP

Performing a dry-clamp run before glue-up allows you to check the fits of parts one last time and to preset your clamps to save precious time during a complicated assembly.

top of the seat panel to do the final trimming of the top front rail. Afterward, scrape or sand away any machine marks. Last, pare away the feathered edge where the curve of the rail meets the seat panel (see "Rail Curve Transition").

11. Glue the plugs into the legs, aligning the grain to match that on the rail.

12. Glue the side drawer runners in place. Align the outermost runners with the inside faces of the legs. If you simply screw the center runner in place, you can remove it later for adjustments if necessary.

Constructing the Drawers

Turner constructed his drawers with through dovetails at the corners and then screwed solid cherry drawer fronts to the poplar boxes (see "Drawer"). Alternatively, you could attach the fronts with half-blind dovetails (see "Dovetailed Drawer Construction" on p. 113).

Make the parts

1. Plane, rip, and crosscut the drawer box pieces to size. For the best fit, size the drawer parts to fit their openings exactly. After assembly, you'll handplane or sand the boxes for a snug, but easy sliding, fit.

2. Saw the ⅜-in.-wide by ¼-in.-deep bottom grooves in the sides and box fronts. The grooves sit ⅜ in. up from the bottom edges of the sides and front.

3. Lay out and cut the drawer box corner joints, as explained for the bed pedestal (p. 108). Four tails for each front joint and three tails for each rear joint is about right.

4. Assemble the drawers on a flat surface, insert the bottoms, and compare the diagonals to ensure that the boxes are square under clamp pressure.

5. Sand the drawer boxes and ease the edges and corners with 150-grit sandpaper.

6. Test the fit of the boxes in their openings. If they're tight, plane or belt sand the sides until the drawer slides easily without racking.

Fit the drawer fronts

1. In preparation for fitting the drawer fronts, clamp stop blocks to the runners so that the front of the box is ¾ in. back from the face of the front rails.

2. Make the drawer fronts, sizing them to tightly fit within the drawer openings; then set them in place. Using a pencil and ruler, draw a cut line around the edge of each drawer front to create a gap of about 1/32 in. all around. Then trim to the cut line.

3. Drill the ½-in.-diameter holes squarely through the drawer fronts to accept the pulls, as shown in the drawing on p. 141.

4. Apply several pieces of double-sided tape to the drawer box fronts; then place the drawer front in its opening. Shim the front until there is a consistent gap all around, then press the front firmly against the tape.

5. Carefully slide the drawer out and clamp the front to the box. Attach the front with a couple of screws from inside the drawer. Next, reinsert the drawer to check the fit. Make any necessary adjustments and then drive home the remaining screws.

6. Line up the drawer fronts flush with the front rails; then glue on a couple of small blocks of wood behind each drawer front to serve as stops, as shown in the drawing on p. 140.

7. Turn the pulls (see "Pull Detail").

Finishing Up

1. Do any necessary touch-up sanding with 220-grit sandpaper. Turner raised the grain afterward with a damp cloth and then resanded with 320-grit paper.

2. Apply the finish of your choice. Turner applied a coat of oil, rubbing it out with 0000 steel wool. He finished up with two coats of a polyurethane gel varnish, scrubbing with 0000 steel wood between coats. Be careful not to spill finish into the drawer-pull holes. If you finish the drawer boxes, use shellac rather than oil, which would smell for some time afterward.

3. Glue the pulls into their holes.

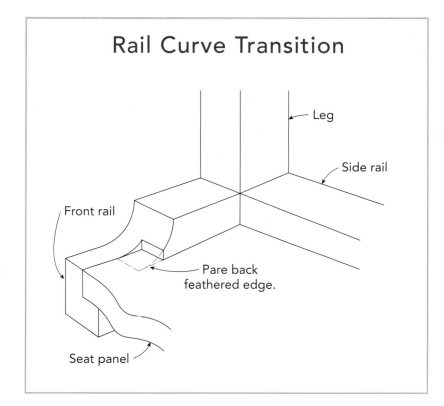

Rail Curve Transition

Leg

Side rail

Front rail

Pare back feathered edge.

Seat panel

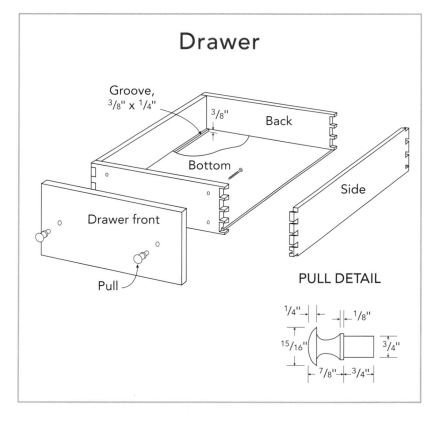

Drawer

Groove, 3/8" x 1/4"

3/8"

Back

Bottom

Side

Drawer front

Pull

PULL DETAIL

1/4"

1/8"

15/16"

3/4"

7/8"

3/4"

MEDICINE CABINET

MOST MEDICINE CABINETS are not designed to safely and discreetly store medicines. The drugs typically sit on shelves within the grasp of youngsters and within plain view of anyone who decides to take an interest in them. Kids are notoriously fascinated by anything that looks like candy, and childproof bottles won't necessarily keep kids out. In another vein, some surveys report that as many as half the visitors to a home snoop in the medicine cabinet.

With this in mind (not that I *personally* have anything to hide), I designed this snoop-proof medicine cabinet with a lockable compartment. For easy access, the compartment can stay unlocked most of the time—its door held shut with a ball catch. But for security, a half-mortise lock can easily be activated with a key. For protection against key scratches, I installed an inset escutcheon. The drop-down compartment door is installed with knife hinges, which are low-profile and perfect for this particular application.

I used spalted sycamore for my cabinet, but any wood will do. You may want to use something that matches your existing cabinetry. The door stiles are a bit proud of the rails, lending visual interest to the door joints. The pulls are made of wenge, but another contrasting wood could work nicely too.

MEDICINE CABINET

The case corners are joined with rabbet-and-dado joints. The back sits in a rabbet routed into the rear edges. The fold-down compartment door, which is recessed ¼" from the case front, is attached with knife hinges, and a half-mortise lock secures the door when desired. The door stiles and rails connect with mortise-and-tenon joints. The mirror sits in a rabbet, held in place with stop strips tacked into the frame.

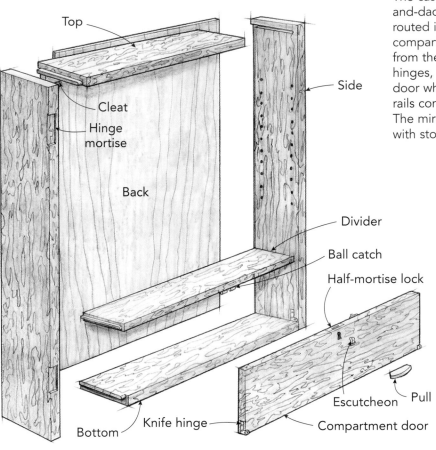

Top

Cleat

Hinge mortise

Back

Side

Divider

Ball catch

Half-mortise lock

Bottom

Knife hinge

Escutcheon

Pull

Compartment door

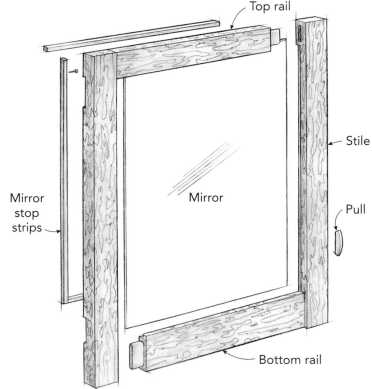

Top rail

Stile

Mirror stop strips

Mirror

Pull

Bottom rail

DESIGN OPTIONS

✦ Make the cabinet longer, wider, or deeper as desired.

✦ Recess the cabinet case into the wall between studs.

✦ Use wooden shelves instead of glass.

Front, Side, and Top Views

FRONT VIEW

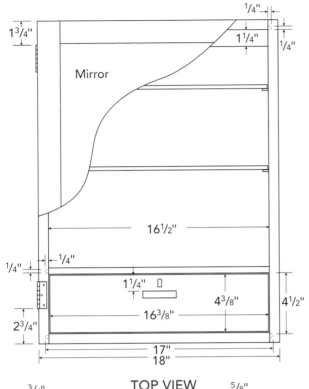

Mirror

1 3/4"
1/4"
1 1/4"
1/4"
16 1/2"
1/4"
1/4"
1 1/4"
16 3/8"
4 3/8"
4 1/2"
2 3/4"
17"
18"

SIDE VIEW (side removed)

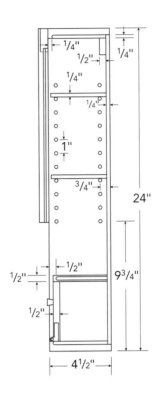

1/4"
1/4"
1/2"
1/4"
1/4"
1"
3/4"
24"
1/2"
1/2"
9 3/4"
1/2"
4 1/2"

TOP VIEW

3/4"
5/8"

FRONT VIEW

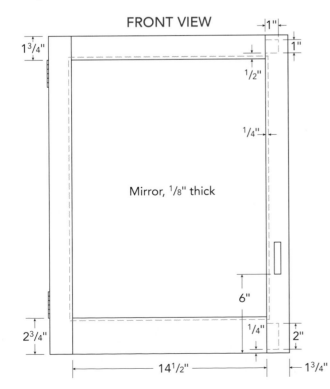

1 3/4"
1"
1"
1/2"
1/4"
Mirror, 1/8" thick
6"
1/4"
2 3/4"
2"
14 1/2"
1 3/4"

SIDE VIEW (stile removed)

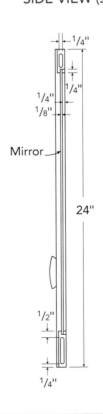

1/4"
1/4"
1/4"
1/8"
Mirror
24"
1/2"
1/4"

CUT LIST FOR MEDICINE CABINET

Case

2	Sides	¾" x 4½" x 24"	solid wood
2	Top/bottoms	¾" x 4½" x 17"	solid wood
1	Divider	½" x 4" x 17"	solid wood
1	Compartment door	½" x 4⅜" x 16⅜"	solid wood
1	Cleat	½" x 1¼" x 16½"	solid wood
1	Back	¼" x 17" x 23"	hardwood plywood

Door

1	Top rail	⅝" x 1¾" x 16½"	solid wood
1	Bottom rail	⅝" x 2¾" x 16½"	solid wood
2	Stiles	¾" x 1¾" x 24"	solid wood
2	Stop strips	¼" x ¼" x 14½"	solid wood
2	Stop strips	¼" x ¼" x 20"	solid wood
2	Pulls	½" x ½" x ½"	solid wood

Other materials

2	Extruded hinges	2½" x 1½"	*from* Woodcraft; item #16Q51
2	Knife hinge	⅝" (offset 1⅜")	*from* Lee Valley; item #01B1415
1	Extruded escutcheon	½" (inside height)	*from* Lee Valley; item #00A03.01
1	Cupboard lock	2" (standard cut)	*from* Lee Valley; item #00P2920
2	Ball catch	1¾" x ⁵⁄₁₆"	*from* Rockler; item #28613
1	Mirror	distance between rabbets minus ¹⁄₁₆"	
2	Shelves (glass)	¼" x 4" x 16⅜"	
8	Shelf support pins	¼" (flat spoon style)	*from* Woodcraft; item #27I11

TIP

If you don't have a screwdriver short enough to fit in a tight space, you can use a power driver tip, turning it with a small wrench.

BUILD THE CASE FIRST; then I fit the compartment door and install the half-mortise lock. After that, I make the cabinet door, fit the hinges, apply finish, install the mirror, and hang the door.

Constructing the Case

Mill the pieces and cut the joints

1. Lay out the case pieces. Next, joint, plane, and saw them to size.

2. Lay out the ¼-in.-wide stopped dadoes on the sides. Note that the top and bottom dadoes stop ¼ in. from the case front and the divider dado stops ½ in. from the case front.

3. Rout the dadoes. I guide the router with a shopmade fence (see photo A on p. 38).

4. Cut the rabbets in the top and bottom pieces to create the ¼-in. by ¼-in. tongues to fit in the case dadoes. I fit my saw with a dado blade and auxiliary fence and then cut the rabbets with the stock lying flat on the saw table (see photo A on p. 73). Back the pieces up with a miter gauge for safe feeding.

5. Leaving the rip fence set where it is, drop the blade to saw the opposing ⅛-in.-deep rabbets that create the tongue on each end of the divider. Begin with the blade set lower than you need and cut both rabbets. Test the fit; then raise the blade a bit and try again. Creep up on the final cuts for a snug fit in the divider dadoes.

6. Raise the blade to ⅜ in. high and saw off the front section of each tongue on all of the pieces.

7. Rout the ¼-in. by ¼-in. rabbets in the rear edges of the top, bottom, and sides. I did this on the router table using a ⁵⁄₁₆-in.-diameter straight bit and laying the workpieces flat on the table. Make sure to stop the case side rabbets ½ in. from the ends of the sides.

Cut the knife hinge mortises

The knife hinge mortises need to be cut in the case sides before assembly, because it would be difficult to do afterward.

PHOTO A: Bore a hole to accept the knife hinge knuckle. Make the hole as deep as the hinge leaf is thick.

1. Dry-assemble the top and bottom to the sides, leaving the divider out.

2. One leaf of each hinge has a pin and one doesn't. Using the pinless leaf, lay out the hinge mortises. Place the knuckle ¹⁄₁₆ in. back from the case front and pressed against the case bottom (see "Medicine Compartment"). Trace around the hinge and inside the pin hole with a sharp pencil. Mark the center of the pin hole with a small awl.

3. Using a ⁵⁄₁₆-in.-diameter brad-point drill bit in the drill press, bore a ⅛-in.-deep hole for the knuckle recess (see **photo A**).

4. Using a ¼-in.-diameter straight bit, rout the majority of the waste from the rest of the mortise (see **photo B** on p. 164). Stay clear of the layout lines.

5. Using a razor-sharp chisel, pare back to the layout lines, testing the fit of the leaf as you go (see **photo C** on p. 164).

6. Drill the pilot holes for the screws now, as it will be difficult to maneuver a drill in the case corner after assembly.

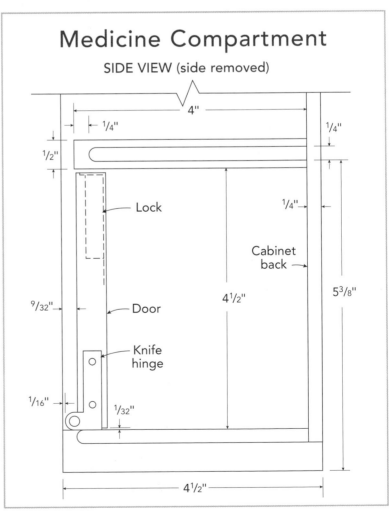

Medicine Compartment

SIDE VIEW (side removed)

Lock

Cabinet back

Door

Knife hinge

4"

¼"

¼"

½"

¼"

5³⁄₈"

4½"

⁹⁄₃₂"

¹⁄₁₆"

¹⁄₃₂"

4½"

PHOTO B: Rout away most of the waste to the depth of the hole while staying clear of the layout lines.

PHOTO C: Using a sharp chisel, gradually pare to the layout lines, until the hinge leaf fits very snugly.

Assemble the case and install the cleat

1. Dry-clamp the case together to check the joint fit and to rehearse your assembly procedures. Lay the case flat on the bench and use cauls to distribute pressure evenly across the joints. Make the back and place it into its rabbets to square up the case before applying the last clamp to the divider (see **photo D**).

2. Glue the case together; then immediately wipe away any glue squeeze-out with a clean, wet rag.

3. After the glue dries, make and fit the cleat and glue it to the case top.

4. Drill the shelf-pin holes using a thick, prebored plywood template. If you prefer, you could lay out the holes on the case sides and drill them on the drill press before assembling the case, but I find template drilling more accurate.

5. Plane the front and rear edges of the case flush to each other.

Constructing the Compartment Door

Make and fit the parts

1. Make the flip-down door for the compartment, measuring the compartment opening and subtracting 1⁄16 in. from the height and width to determine the size of the door. Use quartersawn stock, if possible, to minimize potential warpage (see "Stability Is in the Cut" on p. 8).

2. Lay out the knife hinge mortise in each end of the door. The lower end of each hinge should project 1⁄32 in. beyond the door's bottom edge, as shown in the drawing on p. 163.

3. After adjusting your router bit depth to the thickness of the hinge leaf, rout away most of the waste (see **photo E** on p. 166).

Then pare to the layout lines (see **photo F** on p. 166).

4. Drill the pilot holes and prethread them using a steel screw that matches the size of the hinge's brass screws.

5. Test-fit the doors after attaching the case half of each hinge to the case. Screw one door leaf to the door and hang the other door leaf on its mating leaf. Slip the installed leaves together; then slide the uninstalled door leaf into its mortise and screw it in place.

6. With the door installed, check the gaps around it. Mark cut lines to correct any inconsistencies in the gap, remove the door, and plane to the cut lines. Afterward, reinstall the door, recheck its fit, and make any final corrections in the same manner.

Install the escutcheon, lock, and catch

1. Install the inset escutcheon (see "Installing an Inset Escutcheon" on p. 167). Alternatively, you could tack on a surface-mount escutcheon after installing the lock.

2. Install the half-mortise lock (see "Installing a Half-Mortise Lock" on p. 169). When routing the lock body mortise, use a carbide bit because you'll be cutting partially into the brass escutcheon.

3. Rout the mortise for the lock bolt using a slot-cutting bit (see **photo G** on p. 168). To determine the distance of the mortise from the front edge of the divider, measure from the front of the to door to the front of the bolt and add ½ in.

4. Install the ball catch after replacing the stock springs with springs from a ball-point pen. I attach the pronged half of the catch to the door, lock the door, press the case half of the catch onto the prong, and then mark the screw holes (see **photo H** on p. 168). Drill the pilot holes using a right-angle drill attachment (see photo G on p. 31).

5. Prethread the pilot holes using a ⅜-in.-long steel screw; then attach the case half of the catch in place with brass screws. The brass screws that came with my catch were too long, so I ground them down to ⅜ in. long on my bench grinder.

PHOTO D: Before gluing up the case, do a dry-fit to check your joints and rehearse your clamping procedures. The back, cut to fit tightly in its rabbets, helps hold the case square while the glue cures.

TIP

Don't fret if you rout a hinge mortise a bit too deep. You can simply shim the hinge during installation. Masking tape, business cards, and playing cards all make great shims.

PHOTO E: Clamp the end of the compartment door flush to the benchtop for routing the majority of the waste from the knife hinge mortise.

Constructing the Cabinet Door

The rails are thinner than the stiles on this door, which creates "stepped" joints—adding visual interest to the frame. Keep the different thicknesses in mind as you mill the stock and lay out the joints.

Prepare the pieces

1. Mill the pieces and cut them to length. Make the stiles ½ in. oversize in width and length. That way, you'll later be able to trim the slightly oversize door to fit the case exactly. Mill a bit of extra rail stock for saw setups when cutting the tenons.

2. Lay the pieces out for pleasing grain orientation (see "Grain Layout" on p. 17).

3. Lay out the mortise lengths on the stiles. Then lay out the width of one mortise to use as a reference for setting your router edge guide. The ¼-in.-wide mortises are inset ³⁄₁₆ in. from the back side of the stiles.

4. Using a router edge guide, rout the 1-in.-deep mortises in the stiles.

PHOTO F: Complete the mortise by paring to the layout lines. Notice that the knuckle will project beyond the face of the door.

INSTALLING AN INSET ESCUTCHEON

Although many styles of surface-mount keyhole escutcheons are available, I prefer the subtle elegance of an inset escutcheon. This keyhole-shaped piece of extruded brass fits into a mortise rather than being tacked onto the workpiece like typical surface-mount escutcheons. Fit an inset escutcheon before installing the lock.

1. Locate the position of the lock pin on the door; then drill a hole that matches the outside diameter of the round escutcheon head. Use a brad-point bit to prevent tearout and drill to a depth about ½₂ in. less than the depth of the escutcheon.

2. Clamp the escutcheon in place over the hole, with its tapered side down. Trace around the skirted area using a very sharp knife.

3. Remove the waste in the skirted area using a razor-sharp chisel. Cut only to the depth of the drilled hole (see photo below). Work carefully, test-fitting the escutcheon occasionally without pressing it in completely.

4. Line the walls of the mortise with a mixture of sanding dust and epoxy or cyanoacrylate glue; then clamp the escutcheon in place with waxed paper on top of it.

5. After the adhesive has cured, sand the surface flush.

6. Using a bit that matches the inside diameter of the escutcheon head, bore a hole completely through the door.

7. After installing the lock, saw away the waste in the skirted area using a coping saw.

5. Saw the tenons. I do this with a dado blade on the table saw, first cutting the ³⁄₁₆-in. by 1-in. rabbet on the back side of each rail. Next, I adjust the height of the dado blade and cut the rabbets on the face side (see **photo I** on p. 170). Adjust the blade height again to cut the ¼-in. and ½-in. shoulders.
6. File and pare the edges of the tenons to approximately match the radius of the mortise.
7. Sand the faces and inside edges of the rails and stiles through 220 grit, rounding the edges gently. Then apply one coat of fin-ish to the faces and interior edges of the rails, and to the area adjacent to the mortises. This will make removal of excess glue at the stepped joints much easier later.

Assemble the door
1. Dry-fit the door to make sure the joints fit well and that they clamp up squarely and lie flat on the bench. If not, make any necessary adjustments.
2. Glue and clamp the door, making sure it's flat on the bench and that the clamp screws are centered across the thickness of the stock

to prevent the pieces from cocking out of alignment.

3. After the glue cures, plane or belt sand the back of the door flat.

4. Rout the ¼-in.-wide by ⅜-in.-deep rabbet in the back side to accept the mirror and stop strips. Chisel the rabbet corners square after routing.

5. Rip the ¼-in. by ¼-in. stop strips to fit.

6. Measure for the mirror by subtracting ¹⁄₁₆ in. from the distance between the rabbet walls. When ordering the mirror, specify that you want it cut accurately. At the same time, order the glass shelves. I had the shelf edges "polished" (or "eased") to round them slightly.

Hang the door

Because this is an overlay door, it's easy to install. You'll cut the hinge mortises, temporarily attach the hinges, and then trim the door flush to the case.

PHOTO G: Use a slot-cutting bit to rout the mortise for the lock bolt. Clamp square scrap to the divider to steady the router. (The masking tape here simply provides a better view of the bit.)

TIP

I love the elegant little brass ball catches used in this cabinet, but their springs can be too strong for a small door like this. No problem. Simply unscrew the spring caps, remove the two springs, and replace them with ball-point pen springs cut to the same length as the stock springs.

PHOTO H: After attaching the pronged half of the ball catch to the door, snap the other half in place from behind the cabinet and mark the screw holes.

INSTALLING A HALF-MORTISE LOCK

Half-mortise locks provide a strong, discreet way to secure doors, drawers, and box lids. Although lock bolt configurations differ depending on the application, the mounting procedure is the same for all the lock bodies. Installation simply requires cutting three different mortises: a large one to accommodate the lock *box* and two shallow ones to recess the thin *backplate* and *selvage*.

1. First, lay out the lock pin location. Measure the backset of the lock—the distance between the outer face of the selvage and the center of the pin. Transfer that distance in from the outer edge of your door and mark the pin location with an awl.

2. Using a brad-point bit that matches the diameter of the keyhole, drill all the way through the door at the pin location. (When using an inset escutcheon, as here, install the escutcheon before this step.)

3. Using a ruler and square, lay out the mortise for the box, positioning it so the lock pin lines up with your drilled hole. Then rout it

about $1/32$ in. deeper than the combined thickness of the box and backplate. Cut the mortise a bit wider and longer than the box; the backplate will cover any gaps.

4. Lay out the mortise for the backplate. First place the box in its mortise, centering the pin side to side in your drilled hole. Score the outline of the backplate onto the door using a sharp knife. Rout out the majority of the waste to a depth that matches the thickness of the backplate. Then pare to your knife lines using a razor-sharp chisel.

5. Lay out the selvage mortise on the edge of the door. Press the lock in its mortises and trace around the selvage with a sharp knife. Rout and chisel the mortise as before.

6. Widen the backplate mortise just enough for the selvage to seat in its mortise. With the selvage pressed into its mortise and the backplate resting on the back of the door, trace the bottom edge of the backplate with a knife; then pare to the lines (see photo above).

7. Using the lock's keyhole opening as a guide for size, lay out the skirted section of the keyhole, flaring the edges out a few degrees. Then cut the shape with a coping saw and screw the lock in place.

A HALF-MORTISE LOCK

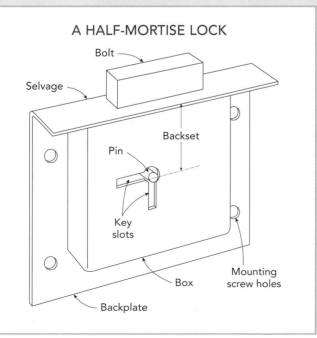

Bolt

Selvage

Backset

Pin

Key slots

Mounting screw holes

Box

Backplate

PHOTO I: To saw tenons with a dado blade, use the rip fence as a stop block and back up narrow workpieces with the miter gauge for safe feeding. For long tenons that require more than one pass over the blade, cut the waste at the end first, moving toward the tenon shoulder in subsequent passes.

Pulls

FRONT VIEW

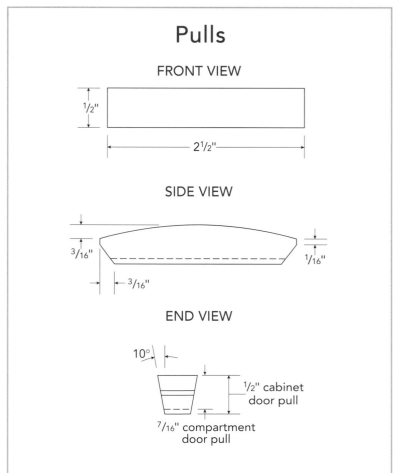

1/2"

2 1/2"

SIDE VIEW

3/16"

1/16"

3/16"

END VIEW

10°

1/2" cabinet door pull

7/16" compartment door pull

1. Clamp the hinges to the case and trace around each leaf with a sharp knife.

2. Outfit your router with a ¼-in.-diameter straight bit and edge guide. Adjust the edge guide for a cut that reaches the far wall of the mortise. If you're using good-quality extruded hinges, as I suggest, adjust the bit depth to the exact thickness of the hinge leaf. If you're using typical stamped hardware store hinges, adjust the bit so it projects about ½₂ in. below the center of the hinge pin, with the hinge lying on the upside down router base (see "Cut the Hinge Mortises in the Case" on p. 59).

3. Rout the case mortises, staying clear of the knife lines on the shorter edges of the mortise (see **photo J**). Afterward, pare to the remaining knife lines with a sharp chisel.

TIP

When tacking in stop strips for mirror or glass, use as small a hammer as possible and lay a piece of corrugated cardboard over the glass in the area that you're working.

4. Install a hinge in each mortise using a single screw. Drill a pilot hole first, offsetting it very slightly so the screw will pull the hinge toward the rear mortise wall.

5. Fold the hinges over and place the door on the case, aligning the hinged side of the door and the case. Split any overlap between the top and bottom evenly. Slide a sharp knife against each edge of a leaf and into the edge of the door to transfer the hinge placement. Then use a square to extend knife lines across the back face of the stile to mark the hinge outlines.

6. Rout and chisel the hinge mortises in the stile as you did in the case; then attach the door to the hinges with one screw only.

7. With the door attached, plane or sand the door edges flush to the case edges.

Make the pulls

1. Lay out the profile of the pulls on ½-in.-thick stock (see "Pulls"). This is a great opportunity to use a bit of that special accent wood you've been hoarding. Note that the compartment pull is ¹⁄₁₆ in. shallower than the door pull.

2. Shape the side profile. I used a disk sander, but you could use a belt sander or scrollsaw.

3. Handplane the 10-degree bevel on each side of the pull; then sand the pulls through 220 grit.

Finishing Up

Sand and apply the finish

1. Remove all of the hardware and sand everything through 220-grit. Then glue the pulls in place.

2. Apply a good water-resistant finish. I rubbed on four coats of wiping varnish (see "A Favorite Finish" on p. 19). I used a small artist's brush to work finish into the shelf-pin holes.

Assemble the cabinet

1. Reinstall the compartment door hinges, lock, and catch.

2. Place the mirror into its rabbets and tack the stop strips in place. I predrill the nail holes to prevent splitting the stops.

3. Hang the door and install a ball catch behind the pull.

4. Nail or staple the back on. Then hang the cabinet, screwing through the cleat into a wall stud. Install the shelf pins and shelves.

PHOTO J: By using the same router edge guide setting when routing the hinge mortises on both the case and the door, you're assured of good door–case alignment.

SOURCES

Suppliers

CONSTANTINE'S
2050 Eastchester Rd.
Bronx, NY 10461
(800) 223-8087
Veneer and veneering supplies

FLAMINGO
Flamingo Specialty
Veneer Company Inc.
356 Glenwood Ave.
East Orange, NJ 07017
(973) 672-7600
(973) 675-7778 FAX
Veneer and veneering supplies

GARRETT WADE
161 Avenue of the Americas
New York, NY 10013
(800) 221-2942
Woodworking tools and supplies

HIGHLAND HARDWARE
1045 N. Highland Ave. NE
Atlanta, GA 30306
(800) 241-6748
*Tools, woodworking supplies,
and finishes*

LEE VALLEY
P.O. Box 1780
Ogdensburg, NY 13669
(800) 871-8158
*Cupboard locks, knife hinges, hard-
ware, tools, and woodworking supplies*

LIE-NIELSEN TOOLWORKS
P.O. Box 9, Route 1
Warren, ME 04864
(800) 327-2520
Exceptional handplanes

ROCKLER
4365 Willow Dr.
Medina, MN 55340
(800) 279-4441
*Hardware, casters, tools, and wood-
working supplies*

WOODCRAFT
P.O. Box 1686
560 Airport Industrial Rd.
Parkersburg, WV 26102
(800) 225-1153
*Hinges, locks, box feet, hardware, tools,
and woodworking supplies*

WOODWORKER'S HARDWARE
P.O. Box 180
Sauk Rapids, MN 56379
(800) 383-0130
*Drawer slides, hanging file rails,
casters, hinges, clothes rods, locks,
catches, pulls, etc.*

WOODWORKER'S SUPPLY
1108 N. Glen Rd.
Casper, WY 82601
(800) 645-9292
*Large dowels, General Finishes Seal-A-
Cell and Arm-R-Seal, hardware, tools,
and woodworking supplies*

Designers

PAUL ANTHONY
Paul Anthony Studios
P.O. Box 386
Riegelsville, PA 18077
*Modular compact disc cabinet, audio-
cassette cabinet, file cabinet, kitchen
work station, and medicine cabinet*

KEN BURTON
Windy Ridge Woodworks
6751 Hollenbach Rd.
New Tripoli, PA 18066
*Desktop organizer, printer stand,
and bed pedestal*

ADOLPH SCHNEIDER
Fine Woodcrafts
495 Olive St.
Alpha, NJ 08865
*Convertible wine cabinet
and pantry door shelves*

ALLEN SPOONER
AMS Custom Woodworking
4 Steven Ave.
Somerville, NJ 08876
Man's jewelry box

DENIS KISSANE
5020-2D Samet Dr.
High Point, NC 27265
Mobile closet

PETER TURNER
Furnituremaker
126 Boothby Ave.
South Portland, ME 04106
Storage bench